The Energy Cure

The Energy Cure

Cure

How to Recharge Your Life
30 Seconds at a Time

Kimberly Kingsley

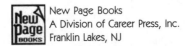
New Page Books
A Division of Career Press, Inc.
Franklin Lakes, NJ

THE ENERGY CURE

EDITED BY KATE HENCHES

TYPESET BY MICHAEL FITZGIBBON

Cover design by Howard Grossman

Printed in the U.S.A. by Book-mart Press

To order this title, please call toll-free 1-800-CAREER-1 (NJ and Canada: 201-848-0310) to order using VISA or MasterCard, or for further information on books from Career Press.

The Career Press, Inc., 3 Tice Road, PO Box 687,
Franklin Lakes, NJ 07417
www.careerpress.com
www.newpagebooks.com

Library of Congress Cataloging-in-Publication Data

Kingsley, Kimberly, 1964-

The Energy cure : how to recharge your life 30 seconds at a time / by Kimberly Kingsley.

p. cm.

Includes bibliographical references and index

ISBN-13: 978-1-56414-963-3 (alk. paper)

ISBN-10: 1-56414-963-3 (alk. paper)

1. Conduct of life. 2. Vitality. 3. Stress (Psychology) 4. Self-help techniques. I. Title.

BF637.C5K555 2008

158.1--dc22

2007017183

To Ann and Roy Kingsley

For demonstrating love, compassion, and brightness every day.

Acknowledgements

My relationship with God is the foundation and inspiration for all my work. My gratitude for this primary relationship in my life transcends words.

"Hearty thanks" to my agent John Willig, who is clearly a bright one in the publishing field, and to Matt Holt, who pointed me in the right direction and graciously answered my questions.

Thank you to everyone at Career Press/New Page Books—a publishing house with great energy.

I would like to thank Hal Zina Bennett for his initial enthusiasm, as well as Barbara Neighbors Deal for her valuable feedback early on.

Special thanks to Bill Lettow for doing the first round of editing, and for his invaluable feedback and friendship.

Thank you to Luis Medina for the "right on" graphic used for the proposal.

Deep gratitude goes to my amazing family and friends for their unwavering support, and for bringing a special sweetness into my life—you know who you are!

And to Michelle, Kristine, and Amy, who brought their energy and light to this project and let me read to them.

Special thanks to Anna Peggie for being who she is and inspiring me every day with her joyful spirit—and to Jimmy Peggie who helps me take good care of her.

And finally, I would like to give a heartfelt thanks to my clients, students, and readers—I celebrate your brightness.

Contents

After a few moments, I was able to see him better. He was an average-looking man with his shirt tucked neatly in his belted jeans. The details of his appearance are irrelevant, for what was powerful enough to make me stop and pay attention was his brightness. We do not always *see* a person's brightness, but we do always *perceive* it. It may be a good feeling that you get, or simply their presence that feels strong to you.

This kind of brightness is the charge that comes from having a strong connection to your internal source of energy. This internal, spiritual energy is life itself—undiluted, unobstructed life. It is what makes one bright. You can be powerful without being spiritually charged; however it is an externally derived power, not bright, and always fleeting.

This book is concerned with internal, authentic, spiritually derived power. We will explore how to plug in to this unlimited source of spiritual energy, and how to manage it in a way that supports your purpose: authentic self-expression.

Your Energy System

The human energy system is like any other system in nature. It is complex and completely interdependent. If one aspect is out of balance, the whole system is compromised. There are many ways we lose energy, and just as many ways to enhance it, but managing your energy is simply a means to an end.

Self-expression is our ultimate goal, and when we manage our energy optimally, we fulfill our functions of self-expression. Life is *pro* creation—in favor of extending itself. Genetic procreation, pollination, and creative endeavors are all ways that life fulfills its most basic function. Realizing and aligning with this fundamental, organic principle is the key to individual fulfillment and success.

It is easy to get in life's way. The goal is to support the life that naturally seeks to extend through us. When we are not busy literally procreating, we engage in creative self-expression. The words *creative* and *expression* make *creation*.

Your creation does not need to be as profound as the Sistine Chapel. It does not even have to be an active process. We express ourselves even when we are not trying. The man at my daughter's school was not doing anything special other than walking to his truck, yet his essence was moving through his body, resulting in a strongly charged energy field—he was bright.

Just as your body does not require you to deliberately digest food, effort is not necessary for life to extend or move through you. What is required is for you to become proficient in the language of energy—your one point of reference. There are many qualities of energy, and discerning these subtle variations will provide you with all the information you need to get out of the way and follow life's lead toward your unique version of nirvana.

Energy Tip: Next time you're in a crowd, look around and see if you notice any Bright Ones. Do you see, feel, or sense the life emanating from them?

The Stress Effect

Modern life is incredible. Our life expectancy is at an all-time high, averaging 77.6 years of age. We are connected to each other as no other time in history. And technology continues to evolve, at what seems like the speed of light.

Although all this is true, there are two sides to every story. One has to wonder if there is such a thing as being over-connected. Is it possible that being connected to each other via the Web and cell phones is leaving us disconnected from ourselves? Are MP3 players, television, and computers taking up so much space in our minds that we are becoming deaf to the more subtle nudges of instinct and intuition? Are we as a society becoming addicted to being plugged in to the outside world? And finally, what are the implications of being chronically disconnected from ourselves?

Childhood and teenage obesity is on the rise. In fact, experts now predict that life expectancy will drop later in this century due to the rise in childhood obesity. Why do people overeat? One reason is because food is grounding. It helps us to feel solid and planted on the ground—perhaps our children need grounding in a world that is moving so fast. The thing is that grounding occurs naturally when we play outside rather than watch television.

Not being plugged in to the present moment is the biggest threat we face in terms of our health. Why is this? Because nourishing, spiritual energy only comes from within. Further, the energy in our bodies sends us messages about how to take care of ourselves all the time, but we can only receive the information if we are tuned in to the present moment. When we are strung out, spread thin, and over-connected with everything except ourselves, we ignore these messages and begin to starve.

It is estimated that 75 to 90 percent of visits to primary care physicians are stress related. If modern life is so easy, why are we so stressed? Perhaps moving at our current pace, for all its advantages, does not give us adequate time to recharge. The bottom line is this: One's ability to cope with everyday challenges directly correlates to the degree that he or she is energized and nourished from within. The principle is the same for

will get louder and louder. Initially, the information you receive will be focused on whatever is blocking life. As you charge, life will naturally want to extend through you and guide you in making decisions that support its increased expression.

When you read the tips in this book and start to notice all the things zapping your energy, don't panic. Just breathe, meditate, or walk—focus on whatever you do to nourish and charge your system with pure spiritual energy. The rest will happen organically and at the pace with which you are most comfortable.

My experience is that the biggest obstacles to core expression come to the surface first. Maybe the first block is a relationship or habit that needs to be transformed or released. It is not practical to tackle everything at once; therefore, follow whatever comes up.

As you read these words, your inner self has probably already revealed your biggest source of energy depletion. If you're not ready to go there yet, don't. Just commit to deliberately receiving spiritual energy daily, and soon you will be ready to take the next step on your journey. It is amazing how quickly we are able to release patterns when we are ready. In the following seven sections we will explore how to spiritually charge from within—the first step toward embodied spirituality.

Ꭶ One Point of Reference

Ꭶ Charge Daily

ᔏ Levels of Self

ᔏ Just Breathe

ᔏ Letting Life Lead

ᔏ Embracing Your Potential

ᔏ Stay Grounded

One Point of Reference

Fully charged people live by the principle that there is only one point of reference for every decision. This point of reference is life energy within you. Life guides us as to how it is best supported. Simply put, there are life-enhancing decisions and life-depleting decisions. Cultivating this frame of reference is how we support self-expression.

Here's the catch: what I find life-enhancing may be depleting for you. For example, I am a writer. Each time I sit down and begin to write, life fills my body and I am joyful. If you are a natural designer or architect, and you sit down to write, energy may drain from you as you struggle to find the right words to express yourself. However, as you pick up a pencil and begin to draw, you may reverse the flow and become charged with energy and enthusiasm.

Therefore, to fulfill your function and to be as charged and life-filled as you can be, you need to develop the habit of checking your energy on an ongoing basis. Even basic questions such as, "Do I eat turkey or roast beef?"

take on new significance from the perspective of managing your energy. Most of the time, the life energy within you prefers one over the other. Traditional wisdom may say that turkey is the healthier choice; however, your body might be better balanced by roast beef on that particular day.

"Should I go to the beach this year for the customary family reunion?" The whole family may shun you if you don't go—however, life might desperately need you to stay home and get organized (and therefore more grounded) during your time off.

This habit of referring to your internal point of reference leads to an increased ability to understand the language of energy. When you ask yourself the question about turkey versus roast beef, does your body perk up or slump down? That's information. Generally speaking, higher vibrations (energy flow without resistance) provide the positive feelings that we love, and feel light and somewhat buoyant, indicating a yes to whatever it is you are asking, whereas a no feels more like a sinking stomach, or subtle heaviness in your being. Proficiency comes with practice and an initial leap of faith. You will quickly learn to trust your ability to sense—almost effortlessly, like dancing—information that supports, rather than obstructs energy flow. Once you experience the increased energy and well-being as a result of honoring life, you will be hooked.

Energy language 101 involves two words: nourishment and depletion. Short-term gratification suddenly takes on a new light—"Is it worth it?" And if the price you pay is energy loss, the answer will be a resounding no. Once you become adept at discerning the voice of life instead of, for example, the voice of your habits, the concept of self-discipline changes from doing what you think you "should" do, to doing what feels best.

Doing what feels best is simple; it does not require constant effort or Olympic-style discipline. Rather, once you get into the groove, it feels more like going with the flow. There is a period of adjustment when you shift from making decisions based on multiple external reference points to a single internal point of reference. You may find parts of you resisting during this adjustment phase, but after that it is smooth sailing.

For example, I often work with women who are addicted to weighing themselves. The number on the scale, the external point of reference, has the power to determine their mood and behavior for the entire day. Due to chemicals in the brain that are released whenever we engage in addictive behavior, weighing themselves provides a small energy boost at first—however, stepping on the scale usually proves to be an overall energy drain. I advise them to stay off the scale, except for annual visits to the doctor, and instead to refer to their appetites and energy in their bodies to guide decision-making. By asking,

"What choice will leave me feeling most buoyant and clear?" you give your body an opportunity to participate, often leading to a much better choice than your mind alone would make.

In addition to physical feelings of lightness and elevation, your emotions provide information as to what's nourishing versus depleting. Joy, peace, and contentment indicate that you have made an energizing choice. If a choice causes irritability, frustration, or guilt, it is depleting!

Energy Tip: Life flows through peaceful corridors—if you want to know which decision supports life, ask yourself if it will give you inner peace. If the answer is yes, then go for it!

The initial resistance many of us experience when letting go and yielding to life comes from a fear of losing control. At some level, we believe that obsessing enough about our actions will put us in control. This is a trap. Surrendering to the will of life is like letting go of a branch on the side of the stream and allowing the water to carry you to your destination—all the while having a blast! It is a loss of control in terms of the ego, the part of us that is strongly identified with form (our bodies, thought forms, habits, and so on), and the ego fights hard to maintain its position. The key to gracefully surrendering to life is to tread lightly. Gently nudge your ego, laugh with it, observe it, and it will eventually yield. If you fight it, you feed it, and it gets stronger.

So if you must get on the scale, do it with lightness and make a joke while you're at it. Tomorrow, you may not feel the need.

Charge Daily

Unless you are spending your days in a quasi-meditative state in a retreat-like setting, you are most likely energy deficient.

The pace of modern life depletes any energy we get from a decent night's sleep by, I'd say, 11 a.m. It is essential that we augment the renewal properties of sleep with daily meditative activity. We will define meditative activity as a period of time when your awareness expands from being primarily in your brain to being in your entire body, allowing for mental stillness. As you experience these intermittent moments with no thoughts, pure life energy has an opportunity to expand beyond your thoughts. Some spiritual teachers, such Deepak Chopra and Wayne Dyer, refer to this mental stillness as "getting in the gap."

Each time you are able to slip into the gap between your thoughts, pure, spiritual energy infuses every cell of your body, including your brain. For me, this feels as though my brain is being reformatted, like a computer disk. All redundant thoughts are wiped away so that my brain is open to serving my higher self instead of the other way around.

This charge of spiritual energy also extends slightly beyond the body, buffering it from the blows of the day. Things such as bad traffic and cranky coworkers simply bounce off a well-charged person, with a blessing going back in his or her direction. You gladly remain unaffected and grounded.

The voice of life gets clearer as well. When you bring more life into your body and clear the cobwebs of erroneous thoughts from your mind, you will more clearly perceive information that supports the flow of life. It feels natural, and not forced. You may, for example, be in the habit of surfing the Web at night as "filler" to a draining day. As more pure energy inhabits your body, you will simply not feel like spending excessive time on the computer. Rather, your body and clear mind might guide you to writing a handwritten letter to your aunt or toward another nourishing activity.

Energy Tip: The next time you head toward that activity that seems to provide a break from daily life, check the feelings in your body before and after the activity to see if it was truly nourishing.

There are many ways to relax into inner expansion and stillness. Some of you will want to create a space for meditation, and sit each morning. This is my daily ritual, though walking in nature is a favorite as well. If you are a mover, feel free to walk or run (go ahead and take your iPod, but make sure you have some time without music, which can be a distraction from self). A gardener? Start digging! The only real requirements are solitude and mental stillness. I am aware, however, that complete solitude is hard to come by. I remember taking a meditation class in downtown Chicago, where the elevated train would roar by about every 10 minutes. Most of us don't have the luxury of escaping to a remote area in the mountains or by the ocean for our daily meditation. Simply cut out television, music, and conversation. People in the immediate vicinity will register in your awareness, so it's best to have a door or some space between you. But we can't ship off our kids or neighbors every time we want to meditate either, so relative solitude and silence will do.

Create your own daily ritual. Leaving it to chance is dangerous; time can easily be filled with a million other things. Pick your time, place, and activity, and go with it. After about 30 days you will find that if you skip, you feel malnourished.

Levels of Self

There are four levels to every human being:

1. Spiritual
2. Emotional

3. Mental

4. Physical

Managing your personal energy in a way that supports the flow of life requires that you understand each of these levels of self, and the role of each in the process of self-expression.

Let's look at the spiritual level. Spirit is the universal, animating force of all living things. It doesn't matter whether a person considers himself spiritual or not. Each of us has an unseen force that animates our cells and departs when we die; this is the spiritual level, our primary energy source. Food provides energy for your body as well; however, it is a secondary energy source. You can feed a dead person a lot of healthy food, but if the spirit has left, it won't do any good.

One can deny or ignore one's spiritual essence and choose to completely focus on the body, thoughts, and possessions, yet it does not change the fact the spiritual level exists.

Most of us start out over-identifying with our bodies. We think we *are* primarily our bodies and spend all our time and energy trying to protect and defend this fragile territory. Directing all this effort toward the "tip of the iceberg" neglects the larger, spiritual part of our identity—the part that animates our being and nourishes our cells. As our identity shifts to include our spiritual

essence, we can surrender and focus on our true function of self-expression rather than fearfully trying to hold
on to a static form.

Feeding your spiritual core daily allows it to grow in
your awareness, thereby building a solid identity that
reflects your whole self. We nurture the relationship with
our spiritual self by spending time daily in meditation
and following the guidance that life or spirit reveals on
a moment-by-moment basis.

Each morning when I wake up, I set my intentions for
the day. My intention is to love and care for myself by nourishing my spirit, honoring my feelings, aligning my mind,
and taking impeccable care of my body. This captures the
role of each level in the process of self-expression. We
feed our spirits (or rather, make time for our spirits to feed
us!), trust our feelings as guideposts, discipline our
thoughts so that they are positive and supportive of who
we are, and take care of our bodies that they might glorify
spirit through authentic self-expression.

Just being aware of these four levels of self helps
you view yourself more holistically. Try scanning your
body on a regular basis to see where the bulk of your
attention is focused. Often you will find it residing above
your shoulders; this becomes an opportunity to breathe
mindfully and redistribute your energy throughout your
body.

Energy Tip: If you find your awareness condensed into the space between your ears, connect to your breath and allow it to move energy into every crevice of your body. You may find that you get fewer headaches!

Just Breathe

Taking full breaths is the most organic way to bring nourishing energy into your body. It's amazing how few of us breathe correctly, and astonishing how much time we spend in "fight or flight" mode. This physiological response is wired into our makeup as a way to quickly utilize energy reserves to deal with a potentially life-threatening situation.

Many of us have subconsciously learned that by putting our bodies in a state of stress we can produce an energy surge to get us through. So we go about our days, breathing shallowly, releasing stress hormones, and "milking" our energy systems.

The price for routinely operating on adrenaline is extremely high. When you squeeze vital energy from your system in a short amount of time, you will be driven to try to replace your reserves with the same immediacy you felt when you blew through your original supply. This urgent need to rapidly replenish drives us to consume junk food, excessive coffee, too many cocktails, and every other quick fix you can imagine. Unfortunately, none of these excesses does the trick. They only provide another immediate boost to be followed by another, yet deeper lull.

This energetic roller coaster is ultimately unfulfilling, and leaves one in a state of chronic energy deficiency. An alternative to a high stress, over-consuming lifestyle is tapping into a steady supply of spiritual nourishment from your daily practice and deep breathing.

> **Energy Tip:** Whenever you feel boredom or emptiness, it is likely a craving for spiritual nourishment. Take some deep breaths and think of it as equivalent to drinking a fresh-squeezed glass of orange juice.

For some, the thought of stepping off the energetic roller coaster sounds a little boring. This reminds me of something I heard Marianne Williamson once say. I'm paraphrasing, but in essence, she said that you don't leave life's drama behind when you embrace spiritual living; you simply experience higher drama. Deep spiritual energy moving through your body provides a feeling that is more exciting than anything we can manufacture or consume in an attempt to feel more alive.

Proper breathing is one of the best ways to keep your system energized throughout the day so that you don't ever go below your reserves and frantically start searching for a quick fix. Most of us are oxygen deprived. There are several reasons for this. The first is breathing too shallowly—rather than inhaling long, full breaths from our diaphragm, we take in short bursts of air from our upper chest.

Another cause of oxygen deficiency is the decreased air quality in the big cities in which many of us live. This is why oxygen bars—places where people can stop and get a shot of oxygen—are popping up in destinations such as Seattle.

I often take a few deep breaths in between seeing clients or any time I feel that my energy is low. It works like magic to help me remain simultaneously calm and energized. I recommend the breathing exercises taught by Dr. Andrew Weil, found in his book *Healthy Aging*, or his audio series on breathing.

Breathing connects you to your spiritual core. After the morning charge, proper breathing is what keeps you infused with life-enhancing energy. Therefore, if you want the calm, clear-headedness you experience during your charging ritual, then continue to breathe deeply and slowly throughout the day.

Letting Life Lead

Life or spiritual energy speaks in a different language than we are used to. It is far more subtle than the superficial thoughts that swim around in your head. Because of the subtle nature of your spiritual voice, it takes practice to perceive. Learning this subtle language is a skill worth cultivating, however, because the information it relays is invaluable. A few things to remember:

⟿ Your spiritual voice or the voice of life is connected to all of life, and is therefore all-knowing. The guidance you receive will support you *and* everyone else on the spiritual level.

⟿ At times you will receive a complete vision or sense of what the future holds, but moment-by-moment direction is the norm. Your spiritual voice will direct you in the present moment, because it is timeless.

⟿ Everyone perceives his or her spiritual voice (the language of life energy) differently. With practice, you will learn a unique set of feelings or symbols that guide you to your highest good. Paying attention to what is nourishing versus depleting is the basis for further energy literacy.

ॐ Each time you honor your spiritual voice it gets louder.

All Knowing

Some people resist developing their intuitive abilities due to a belief that doing what they want is somehow selfish. There is a reason for this thinking—although it is unproductive and false. Before you started relying on your intuition or energy to guide you, others likely had more say in your decisions. Once you begin marching to the beat of your own drum, you may experience resistance from the people closest to you. This is common, and should not discourage you.

Remember, each of us is composed of four levels, so if your inner voice requests more solitude, don't be surprised if your mate, for example, reacts strongly—not on a spiritual level, but on an emotional and physical level. If you are able to see the big picture the way life does, you might see that your spending more time alone will be a catalyst for your mate getting back in touch with a long- lost passion.

Honoring the voice of life sometimes leads to a relationship or a job falling apart. Although painful, these transformations always make room for more energy, and therefore a more fulfilling life.

If you notice people around you staying stuck, remember that your growth is the best inspiration, and that they will yield to life when they can.

Following your own guidance is easier when you keep in mind that your spiritual voice is connected to all of life. You are therefore serving everyone on the deepest level when you heed your own spiritual wisdom.

Present Moment Guidance

Most of us want to know the whole picture, now! Your spiritual voice does not work that way, for the most part. As mentioned previously, occasionally you will get an impression of the future, but consider it a gift, and don't seek that level of information all the time. Life will lead you to your destiny one step at a time. It will also serve all four levels of your being so that you remain balanced. You might think that you need to be working on the next great invention, while your inner voice is just telling you to relax and enjoy the weather.

It's wonderful to take time to frequently dream and envision your ultimate life, but when it comes to taking action, your best bet is to ask your inner self, "What do I do now?" Then assess each choice for feelings of nourishment or depletion. You will be surprised at how quickly these baby steps march you to your destiny. Space and rest are just as important as work, although it is common for us to be hard on ourselves when we are not "being productive."

A client recently came to see me while going through a very painful divorce preceded by 19 years of emotional abuse. She has health problems, and her future is completely unknown until her divorce is settled. She shared that some days she doesn't even take off her pajamas, because her body just wants to cocoon. In the next breath she spoke about how bad she feels for not working.

I reminded her that caterpillars don't work while they turn into butterflies, and that it takes energy to heal and transform. Sometimes the Western work ethic is counterproductive. Being bright calls for constant renewal in which periods of activity are punctuated by stillness. Desire is one of the ways life energy speaks to us. If you desire rest, it is probably because it is the next step, and therefore the most productive thing to do.

The Voice of Life

Beyond being aware of what brings energy into your system and what depletes it, know that as life moves through you it will speak to you in a language you can understand. If you are a feeling person you will probably get "gut feelings" or simply an intuitive sense of what to do. If you have a great mind, you might just know. Some visual people may actually see a picture in their mind's eye; yet others will hear a still. small voice. This is your energy language—you are the only one who understands this language, and should feel confident in your choices even though others may not understand them.

Energy Tip: Try to remember the last time you heeded your intuition or followed a directive given by life. Did the information come from a feeling, a hunch, a voice, or a picture? Write it down and make it a habit to record your impressions in order to accelerate learning your energy language.

Honoring Your Energy Language

Initially, it is common to question the validity of your energy perceptions. Don't fret—as I said, the language is subtle. The good news is that through time you'll get a solid sense of when you perceive a message from life versus when the "message" is just a random thought or perhaps an emotional trigger from your past.

Each time you trust yourself and act on the information you receive, you'll find that the message gets stronger, louder, and clearer. A leap of faith is the first step, and the second, and the third. Sometimes you might be wrong. It's okay. That is how you refine your skill: by taking some risks and making a few mistakes along the way.

Your daily energizing practice clears your inner world so that spiritual energy can flow. I can't stress the importance of daily spiritual practice enough. You can read every book on the spiritual bookshelf and end up a walking library, but daily tending of your spiritual core is necessary for you to experience an increased flow of life and energy.

Hearing and trusting life, as you perceive it, is very natural. In fact, you already do it—a lot—but may not be labeling it as such. Simply set your intention to tune in to this subtle direction, and it will happen even more frequently. In fact, if you tune in to your spiritual self right now, I bet you will think of one thing to do to support the flow of life. Now trust yourself and do it!

Embracing Your Potential

In order to beam like a lighthouse in a storm you need to be willing to live at your spiritual, emotional, mental, and physical potential. Many of us are comfortable with one or two of these levels, but the duty of a Bright One is to radiate from all four.

Embracing your potential is tricky business. We are socialized with a sense of false humility—the feeling that if we are fantastic, we will be too "full of ourselves." It is true that those of us who are charged on all four levels are full of ourselves. Only, it is a fullness that comes from overflowing spiritual essence.

Because we know deep down that we are meant to be full of and expressing life energy, if we get too puffed up on an ego level, it feels fraudulent. Spiritual energy tends to crumble this sort of ego identification, making room for more authentic empowerment.

42

True potential emerges through acceptance of your unique brand of expression. The life that moves through you is universal, yet in form, you are completely unique. This allows the shape and flavor of your individual expression to be different from others, while the essence is the same.

While growing up, many of us pushed parts of ourselves out of sight, not realizing that they contained vital energy and are necessary pieces of the puzzle that is the self. Rejecting any piece of you creates a hole in your energy system that you subconsciously try to fill from the outside in. That is why someone, for example, who has buried his or her inner musician, is consistently attracted to people who are musical. Or perhaps you are sitting on the outspoken part of yourself and you find that you're always in the company of "loudmouths."

Rejected pieces of you create a vortex, a black hole in your energy system attracting the missing piece like a magnet. It can never be filled from outside yourself, but only reclaimed from the inside. Only then will your essence fill that void and extend beyond it, making you feel fulfilled and whole. You will no longer attract from a place of need or incompleteness, but of fullness and integrity.

Unless you are a true free spirit, you have most likely internalized the belief that if you are too different from others you will be rejected. This is an unfortunate aspect of socialization. Just visit a high school to see this in action—kids who are the same are together, and kids who are different are alone. At some point we need to reconcile socialization with spiritual principle. Only when we relax into our uniqueness can we fully contain our core energy.

You have gifts that, when cultivated, accelerate your velocity of self-expression. You are born with this untapped potential, and, through time, begin to perceive it. The unique talents of some people are so pronounced that everyone around them can tell how they will bring their light into the world from a very early age. Others have many talents and could click into any one of them to accelerate their expression.

My mother always says that a child's personality does not change through time. My youngest sister, Kristine, was a bossy, yet loving little girl. She was full of joy, sparkle, and natural strength. Because her innate disposition was appreciated and supported, she grew up to be a diplomatic leader and a compassionate woman—exactly the same, only more refined, as she was at 3 and 4 years old.

On the other hand, Jeannie, who is a client of mine, recently shared her dismay at being introverted. After I reminded her that if she were a social butterfly she probably wouldn't have made it through law school, she admitted her introversion hasn't been all bad. During our discussion, she remembered her mother and father constantly teasing her for not being more social; as a child, Jeannie would often be found in her room reading rather than playing with friends. Had her family chosen to focus on Jeannie's brilliant mind—her natural strength—rather than her shy demeanor, she may have blossomed socially in her own time, and not rejected that part of herself.

Energy Tip: Ask an elder in your family to describe you as a small child. Have you rejected an aspect of your disposition, such as your excitability, or passion for bugs? If so, invite that part of you back into your life and acknowledge yourself every time you let it out to play.

Your potential is not something to strive for—it is already there. You need only relax into it. This is how:

1. Identify your unique personality, gifts, and physical attributes.

2. Appreciate and honor them daily as your individual mode of spiritual expression.

3. Cultivate them and emphasize them, rather than trying to diminish them.

4. Watch your life transform before your very eyes.

One of the greatest problems we face is self-rejection. Any time you reject yourself on any level you are depriving the world of light and yourself of energy. Open up to love, let it move through you, and you will be brighter than you ever imagined.

Stay Grounded

In order for electricity to travel, it must be grounded. If not, there is no clear path for the current to follow. To be fully charged, you too need to remain grounded. And being grounded enough for spiritual energy to move through you at a high speed involves an integration of spirit and matter.

Historically, there has been a split between spirit and matter. At some level we view God as "out there" in the sky somewhere. The idea that we are apart from God is buried deep in the collective consciousness, affecting us all, at some level, regardless of our religious beliefs. Illustrations of this split can be seen everywhere, even in the assumption that light is somehow superior to darkness.

There is a collective notion that matter is dark, dense, animalistic, and at times even "evil," despite the fact that most matter is infused with light! Nature is a wonderful example of light-filled matter. Transcending the belief that we are apart from our source will lead us to become more light-filled as well. Because we view our bodies as matter, the previous connotations subconsciously apply. Therefore, the task of allowing energy to seep into every crack and crevice of your being requires tremendous patience and persistence. Any time you seek to rise above the web of collective energy, it initially feels counterintuitive.

It is culturally more familiar to believe that only spirit is pure, and that the ideal is to actually be this free, pure, wind-like energy, without the confines of a heavy body. My response to this type of thinking is that you can have that experience when you die. For now, your task is to embody spirit so that your cells become so filled with light and energy that you feel tremendous inner freedom, here and now.

Being grounded enough to be a conduit for expressing spiritual energy into the world involves loving your body as much as your spirit—and doing whatever it takes to facilitate the penetration of spiritual energy into your physical body. The merging of spirit and matter requires the ability to tolerate tension.

Joel is a spirited guy. He loves adventure and enjoys a good whiskey in the evening. If Joel goes without adventure or newness in his life for too long, he gets restless. When feeling restless he tends to drink more whiskey, yet he doesn't like himself during those times.

Joel, like many of us, is in the habit of chasing his spirit rather than embodying and expressing it—which would provide sustaining nourishment and internal adventure as opposed to intermittent highs.

For Joel to reverse the flow of energy from "outside in" to "inside out," he would need to temporarily stop feeding himself these habitual energy boosts. But the first, second, and third time he says no to his nightly whiskey he will feel bored and restless—the very feelings he is trying to escape.

If Joel can sit with this lull in energy for long enough, his core energy will begin to bubble up and flow through him from the inside out. He will start to feel good, and realize that he is naturally passionate. Joel will still enjoy adventure and perhaps an occasional whiskey, but will be acutely aware of when he starts to use those things to fill himself up—an indication that he needs to slow down and reconnect with his internal energy source.

By maintaining awareness, patience, and diligence, with time Joel will become authentically charged. The cells of his body will become permeated with energy and light. He will have transformed—dying to his false dependencies and being born again into his real source of passion: life.

Each of us has external dependencies that we rely on for short-term energy boosts. You have likely already thought of one or two things on which you depend for energy, knowing that after the initial rush your energy levels drop even further. Breaking your reliance on these things invokes a deep-down fear of losing control.

I tell my clients, "sit on your hands"—literally, until the craving stops. I heard this somewhere years ago. The idea of sitting on one's hands helps people realize the difficulty of remaining in the tension until an external craving has passed. The few minutes that you stay present with your craving but don't act on it, you feel like your insides are burning. This is because they are. You are literally burning through old energy pockets that block the flow of life through your being—congratulations.

Energy Tip: Bring the light of awareness to anything you pursue compulsively—soon you will identify more with the light than the object, and it will lose its power.

To be well charged means to stop chasing your spirit and sit still long enough for it to penetrate your body. You will then be a grounded conduit for energy to pour through and into the world. Nothing is more exciting.

Chapter 2

Understand the Energy of Feelings

Feelings are so connected that feelings are so connected to spiritual energy that they are nearly one and the same. The relationship between your feelings and your spirit are captured by the familiar idea that emotion is energy in motion. We could just as accurately say that various feelings and emotions result from spiritual energy moving through the body at different rates. When it moves quickly and unobstructed, positive feelings are produced. Likewise, when spiritual energy is blocked or resisted, it takes on a "heavy" quality akin to sadness or anger.

Advice on how to deal with feelings ranges greatly; this is one area in which many of us are misinformed. The most important point, in terms of personal energy management, is that feelings need to be honored and *never* ignored.

Honoring feelings is like a dance that you have to learn for yourself. It is a little tricky because each of us has a unique combination of personality, suppressed emotion, and environmental conditioning. Therefore one person might need to work on containing her feelings more, whereas another might be better served by increasing his emotional expression.

Here are some principles that are universal:

- Feelings vary in vibration, like the colors of a rainbow. It is important to honor all of them, not just the "light" ones.

- All of us have a reservoir of unprocessed emotions that, when triggered, flood the system and cause an irrational reaction.

- Processing old "baggage" is essential for maximum expression of energy.

- All feelings, whether new or old, provide information that, when honored, moves us closer to blinding brightness.

It might be useful to compare your beliefs about feelings to the previous list. I recently had a very intelligent and spiritual woman in my office who believed that her feelings represented the voice of craziness. As a result, she developed an overactive mind that had her running in circles. Once she realized that the information her feelings provided was just as valuable, (and sometimes more than) her thoughts, she was able to drop down and let them guide her. The last time I saw her, she told me that she's experiencing true inner peace for the first time in a long while.

Honoring your feelings does yield inner peace, and is an indication that life is flowing. In this section we will look at the nature of feelings, and ways to honor them in the moment they arise. The topics are:

- ✌ Tears
- ✌ Empathy
- ✌ Projection
- ✌ Containment
- ✌ Transformation
- ✌ Dreams
- ✌ Gut Feelings

Tears

Have you ever noticed that when you get close to the truth, you cry? The year of my spiritual awakening I remember crying all the time. I was living in Chicago, and wouldn't be surprised if the level of Lake Michigan rose a few inches that year with all the tears I shed.

People often come into my office and just start crying. They will say, "I don't know why I am crying…" I do—their blocks are melting. Tears are a wondrous thing. For good reason, people often associate tears with cleansing. Tears are a physical response to overwhelming emotional energy moving through your body.

From time to time a client will say, "See, I didn't cry today," as if I am going to be proud of them for doing a good job. This is about the time that we have the conversation about tears and how we have them to cleanse our psyches and make more room for joy.

I feel sad that our culture discourages boys from crying. I think this is getting better, and that boys and young men are more in tune with their emotions than their older counterparts. It's a good thing that they are, because holding in tears causes anger, anxiety, depression, and addiction.

Where could we possibly store all this emotional energy? How much energy do you think it takes to keep it down? I recently read something that said that perfect peace comes from having nothing to hide. There is no way to have true inner peace if you have to keep emotional energy at bay.

Energy Tip: Be like a baby—cry your eyes out for two minutes. Once you have cleared your frustration and sadness, look around the room in awe and experience the moment anew.

Your body naturally wants to release anything that is blocking the flow of life. It is contrary to nature to hold it in. The price for doing so is high—emotionally and physically. The first thing to do is make sure that your beliefs about feelings and emotion are in alignment with the nature of life. If, as a child, your family told you to stop being such a baby, or to get over it when you cried, you likely need to change your belief system. Simply tell yourself, "I choose to honor my feelings."

Second, now that you're grown and have the ability to censor who and what you let into your psyche, make sure that you surround yourself with people who respect your feelings.

I was once married to an otherwise wonderful man who would become overwhelmed every time I had a feeling other than happiness or joy. I soon found that I had to hide a big part of myself in order to stay in the relationship. Having been committed to a spiritual path for years, I was unable to sustain this for long. Holding in my feelings was causing me to become fragile. Had I not known better, I may have started taking antidepressants and labeled myself "too sensitive."

We are all sensitive. We are sentient beings. When we try to cut off our feelings for fear of being engulfed, we pay a high price. Feelings flow on the current of life—you can't cut off feelings without cutting off part of your energy supply.

Finally, it is the responsibility of each of us to learn to manage our feelings in a productive manner—a way that is respectful to others *and* supportive to our selves. In defense of my former husband, I had not mastered the skill of managing my emotions in the first several years of our marriage. It is something that I subsequently learned, however, and I am grateful for that.

Remember, when the floodgates open you may feel that you will never stop crying, but if you "go with the flow," the old stuff will eventually melt and your crying will diminish. As an open being, you will continue to have tears from time to time, and hopefully you will be able to view them as the sacred droplets that they are.

Empathy

Have you ever wondered why some people are unable to have compassion for your feelings? Empathy is the ability to emotionally put your self in another person's shoes.

It is not necessary to have experienced the exact situation as the person for whom you have empathy, but it is essential that you have access to similar feelings that arise through the course of your own life experiences.

Empathy is a visceral experience—more instinct than intelligence. If you are open and have access to the entire spectrum of feelings, your body will naturally resonate with another who is experiencing a strong feeling. At times, this spontaneous emotional contagion can occur when you do not intend empathy. Have you ever walked into a room in which two people are having an argument and your body immediately goes tense? Or, you get tearful when someone you love is sad and crying? This happens to many parents—it is what makes having children so enriching, yet at times heartbreaking.

Empathy occurs naturally when we are in touch with our feelings. If someone is unable to empathize with you, it is because they have difficulty embracing their own feelings. Often, a person will be able to resonate with one emotion but not another.

For example, a friend might be great at empathizing with your sadness, but when something fantastic happens, she is unable to celebrate joyfully with you. In this case, your friend is sitting on her own joy, so it is physically impossible for her to access the feeling and share it with you.

On the other side of the spectrum, you may have people in your life who are great with positive feelings, but when you are trying to process something heavy, they're nowhere to be found. Don't take it personally,— your friends likely have some repressed sadness and anger that is trying to surface and clear. If they get to close to anyone who is sad or angry, overwhelming feelings of their own threaten to surface. They may respond by physically retreating, or by minimizing your pain as a way to stay clear of their own.

As someone committed to being a light in this world, you will experience many different feelings. After processing old stuff, you will predominantly feel happiness and joy. When you do feel sadness or anger, you will use it as a guide to act appropriately. Honoring your feelings by taking action when necessary will allow them to clear faster so that you can quickly return to a joyful state.

The worst thing we can do is judge our feelings. They are there for a reason—trust that. You may want to watch how much time you spend around people with limited emotional literacy. Often, we can process feelings autonomously, but occasionally we need to share them with someone. The healing power of a witness is found in the sharing. A moment of empathy and a few supportive words does wonders for stuck emotions that are trying to move through your system.

Finally, you will want to develop the skill of emotional discernment. You can ask yourself, "Is this feeling mine or theirs?" Once you are clear on where it is coming from, you can use selective empathy and guard yourself from free-floating aggression that doesn't belong to you.

Energy Tip: Visualize yourself as a full well of pure water. Each time someone attempts to dump toxic waste into your well, shield it with a lid and let the waste bounce off. Being the recipient of "dumping" serves no one.

It always amazes me when I hear someone talk about how bad their day was because of traffic. There is nothing more wasteful than picking up the energy of road rage. Emotional discernment will help you identify what you are feeling and allow it to bounce off when it's random and not useful for you to feel it. When we feel random negative energy for longer than the split second that it takes to reject it, we feed darkness and negativity rather than expressing refreshing light-filled energy into the environment. Bottom line: empathize wisely.

Projection

Projection is the psyche's greatest trick. It is a brilliant defense mechanism that enables one to be unaware of suppressed emotional energy by placing it onto another person whenever it threatens to come into awareness. It is sophisticated and slick, fooling just about everyone.

Projection keeps denial in place, leading us to think that life is easier because of it. The truth is that we all have unprocessed emotional energy stored in our systems, and as a result are a bunch of walking land mines.

You know when someone treads on one of your mines. You explode inside—and sometimes outside too. You tell them that they are being ridiculous and that they are entirely wrong, and how dare they make such a blatantly incorrect accusation. Bingo—you've been had. Think of an inner land mine as pockets of buried emotional energy that become activated when a similar emotion is generated from a current situation.

These hotspots severely compromise our energy systems. On a subconscious level we are aware of them—as are our loved ones—so we tiptoe around the dangerous territory, hoping not to stumble upon a buried pocket of explosive energy, should a battle ensue—or worse yet, a war. This fragile inner landscape impedes the flow of life energy—authentic self-expression. As you know, when you do not express your essence you are not properly nourished. Feeling hungry, you over-consume, overwork, and numb out, producing disastrous effects on your well-being and energy flow.

If inner freedom, fulfillment, and bright self-expression are among your goals, it is time to pull a "Dr. Phil" and "get real" with your projections. If you're ready to look at what's there—and it is never a pretty sight—then you have taken the most important step.

All you have to do to identify your land mines is to think about your interactions with others. If you have an angry outburst and get over it pretty quickly, projection probably isn't involved. Spontaneous feelings of frustration, sadness, and anger are a natural part of life. Often, just expressing these minor annoyances is enough to get them moving through and out of your system.

It is also normal to be devastated or outraged when you are abused, betrayed, or seriously neglected.

Feelings—whether they arise from projection or not—should never be dismissed as trivial or unimportant.

Projection is sticky and holds on like grease on the bottom of a shoe. Most of the time old emotional residue, the fuel of projection, gets mixed in with spontaneous and appropriate feelings that occur in response to a situation. This mixing can be confusing because you know that something occurred that you don't appreciate, yet your reaction is severe, and you feel unable to efficiently process the incident and move on. This is your opportunity to identify one of your land mines and to clear it out of your system. Simply be still and ask yourself when you have felt similar feelings in the past—ideally the first time and subsequent times—as it might have built up throughout a series of incidents. You may or may not remember anything; either way, we deal with similar, intense, and often suppressed emotions the same way over and over again. Old or not, feel the feelings, because the only way to release them is to experience them as they move through you. Cry, punch a pillow, journal, walk, or do whatever you need to do to feel that old yucky pain—short of exploding onto another person.

Once you have processed some of the old stuff, you will more clearly see what you need to do to move through the current incident. The key here is to give yourself time to reflect on from where your reaction is coming, and *feel* old feelings prior to sorting the situation out with another person. If you try to project your old stuff, along with your current and appropriate feelings, onto someone else, they will reject all of it, and it will take longer to resolve the problem. Distinguishing what's old and what's new will facilitate processing on both ends.

In a spiritually supportive relationship, you will be able to be honest and vulnerable about your land mines that get triggered in the heat of an argument. Your partner, family member, or friend will extend compassion and seek to help you during these times—as they will require your support with their own set of land mines.

Cultivating an awareness of each other's sensitive areas not only builds compassion, but also alleviates some of the tendency to take the reaction personally.

Energy Tip: Emotional energy takes time to dissipate. Allow yourself to feel unresolved for a time, despite the discomfort this entails. In the end, you will have created more room for pure spiritual energy.

If you feel that you would benefit from more information on the nature of projections and clearing out emotional residue, the following books explore the topic further: *Emotional Clearing* by John Ruskan, *Dark Side of the Light Chasers* by Debbie Ford, and my book, *Opening to Life.*

Containment

Emotional energy sometimes takes over, feeling like the blast from a rocket propelling into space. It is intense, at times uncomfortable, and extremely powerful. Learning to balance emotional containment with expression can transform volatile emotional energy into a refined, powerful force that propels you higher and higher toward your dreams.

Many of us have not cultivated the capacity or resilience to contain intense emotions. Rather, we vacillate between undisciplined outbursts and suppression. Why is it important to contain the energy when self-expression is our function?

Welcome to the paradoxical nature of emotional energy—energy in motion. There are cases when it is more appropriate to contain yourself for a time. One such instance is when you are processing old emotions or pulling back a projection.

Let's say that you have an emotional land mine labeled "Abandonment." You've come home from work after a really bad day and want to talk with your significant other about what happened. He is sitting in front of the television watching a basketball game, giving you an occasional "Wow…" when hearing some extra inflection in your voice.

All of a sudden you become enraged (an old land mine has been stepped on)—thoughts race through your head about how he is never there for you, and that he is a selfish, narcissistic son of a baboon. You say a few choice words and storm off.

After being in another room for about 10 seconds you decide to march right back into the living room, turn off the television *for* him, and give him a piece of your mind. BEEP: wrong answer.

This is precisely when you want to exercise your containment muscles. At least until the emotional volcano stops erupting and you can see colors other than red. The truth is that this incident gets activated every time you feel emotionally abandoned. The current trigger is a carefully orchestrated attempt by the universe to help you clear out old stuff, which compromises your innate ability to experience joy. You certainly don't have to take the opportunity presented to you. It will come again and again until you are ready. For the sake of optimism, let's assume you are ready.

The only problem is that you truly feel like you're going to explode, and that if you don't get back in there soon to "blow of some steam" there will be nothing left of you—nevermind exercising your containment muscle...

The burning sensation that you feel when you don't explode is literally transforming old, dense energy into a lighter vibration so that it can move through you and release. The good news is that this is real, and that once you sit through one of these episodes you have increased your capacity to contain not only powerful emotional energy, but also pure spiritual energy, which is your most fundamental source of nourishment. The bad news is that it usually takes half a dozen times or more for all of the old stuff to clear.

You will, however, feel better after the very first clearing session, and once you know that your misery has a higher purpose, it is not as difficult to endure. The amount of time it takes to burn through a layer of emotional congestion varies. Some people experience it for five or 10 minutes, and then they can go talk it out reasonably. Other times you may feel tension for several days as something works its way through your system.

Recently, I was talking with a client who shared that she felt very tense for three days prior to coming in to see me. She intuitively knew her only choice was to simply endure the discomfort by not talking about it or distracting herself from it with compulsive eating or shopping. Sure enough, after three days the feeling lifted, and she was left with the huge realization that she had been displacing her personal power by trying to control circumstances around her. She now feels clear in the fact that she need only focus her energy on managing herself. It took her three days of uncomfortable containment to bring her personal power and energy back into her body where it belongs.

Now that she has emerged from the fog of confusion, she has clarity and vitality that only comes from containing that which needs to be transmuted or refined to the point that it can be processed and released.

Chronically containing your emotional energy is a bad idea. It really is intended to move and not get stuck. The goal is to cultivate the right balance of containment and expression.

Energy Tip: When you are confused, wait. Confusion is a sign that energy is shifting internally. Once it has sufficiently shifted, it will settle, and you will know what to do next.

I have observed a continuum with extreme emotional containment on one end and extreme expression on the other. About half of us over-express and therefore need to learn how to better contain our emotions in order to more effectively process and move on. The other half of the population falls on the under-expressing side of the continuum. These are the people who hold feelings in and would benefit from increased expression. Regardless of where you fall, it will be initially uncomfortable to bring yourself in better balance. Once you do, however, you will find that you process emotions more efficiently, and that the old stuff can clear, making room for more light and pure spiritual energy to permeate your cells.

Transformation

True transformation involves a cellular change. The word *transformation* carries a positive connotation, and it should, but for all the good that comes out of transformation, it also brings gut-level fear, and, at times, even terror.

I recently read that when a caterpillar goes into its cocoon it turns into a transparent, formless substance before taking on the form of a butterfly. Luckily for the caterpillar, it doesn't have this awareness, or it would cling to the ground for dear life, the way we do when we sense transformation on the horizon.

Transformation is a form of death and rebirth. It is for this reason that fear takes hold as one gets closer to entering the unknown—our version of the caterpillar's chrysalis. We feel that our lives are unraveling before our eyes. At the same time, rebirth is nowhere in sight. Transformation involves a complete leap of faith.

There are three stages of transformation:

1. Entry: stepping into unknown territory, "a leap of faith."

2. Chaos: a crumbling of old mental patterns, dissolving emotional energy, and a sense of confusion and discomfort as spiritual energy embarks on a holistic "re-organization."

3. Emergence: a new lease on life. More
    energy in your body, feelings of joy, and
    clarity of mind. Colors are brighter and you
    feel reborn.

Unfortunately, you cannot get to step three without going through steps one and two. Transformation is nothing more than spiritual energy breaking up old patterns so that it can flow more freely. Without knowing the stages of transformation and experiencing the conviction that you will be better for it on the other side, it is easy to run away from fear of the unknown and resist the process. The resistance causes life to become acutely uncomfortable.

Say, for example, that you have a job that you hate. It pays well, however, and has good benefits. You keep noticing what could be interpreted as "signs" of a different future. Perhaps you see a class advertised in the newspaper on a subject that you are passionate about, or you meet someone who simplified their life to follow his or her heart. You find yourself fantasizing more and more about what life would be like if you took the risk and followed your dreams.

But just as you dive deep into the fantasy of your potential life—you snap out of it. Your logical mind kicks in and reminds you of your retirement account and secure paycheck. You drop your head, continue to go through the motions, and try to forget about it. You're due for a raise anyway...

In the meantime, conflicts at work become more frequent. You can hardly stand going to the office, and require at least two Snickers bars each day to get you through. You persevere, knowing (in your rational mind) that it is the responsible thing to do. Several months later your boss comes into your office and tells you that they have to "let you go" due to budget constraints.

Enter the chaotic stage of transformation. This is the difficult way to approach transformation—the path of resistance. You drag your heels until the universe pulls the rug right out from under your feet.

There is another way, and that is to put your trust in life and let it lead. Your spiritual energy knows what it needs in order to increase the breadth and depth of its expression. The first time you go through a full transformation is the most frightening, After that, you know you will be okay, and that if you go with the flow, you will get there faster.

The call for transformation occurs when your everyday choices accumulate to create internal mental and emotional patterns that limit life's expression. After a time, the pressure of built-up energy cracks these rigid patterns, causing them to crumble. Trust this: Know that life has your well-being in mind, and that it will take your hand and walk you through the process, one step at a time.

Energy Tip: Commit to transformation as a way of life. Literally sit down and tell your higher self that you wish to flow with your essence rather than cling to any particular form. Your higher self will remember your commitment even when you don't.

Some people experience transformation after the death of a loved one or during a personal health crisis. Some enter a transformation while married, and have the marriage either transform with them or crumble. Others enter it after years in a stale job, as mentioned previously.

You can postpone transformation, and many do. They quickly get another job, just any job, to fill the void after being fired. They have a few drinks every night to numb out and not feel the discomfort. They replace their spouse with someone eerily similar just months after divorcing. Transformation can be exchanged for a life of denial and escape. However, it cannot be delayed forever, for in the end we all go through the ultimate transformation—leaving the physical body—and if you, like the caterpillar, master the delicate art of transformation now, the "grand finale" will be just as natural and expansive.

Dreams

Have you ever gone to sleep peacefully only to wake up crying? What about waking up in the morning so angry that you could scream? Emotional energy moves through you whenever and however it can. Dreams are a wonderful vehicle to process deep, intense, and sometimes very old emotions.

Dreams are multipurpose. In addition to processing old wounds and traumas, they help us clear out remnants of a stressful day. Sometimes they provide an entertaining backdrop to play out your fantasies. And sometimes dreams provide important information that your psyche is unable to perceive in waking hours.

Whatever the purpose, all dreams transport information directly from aspects of yourself that are normally out of conscious awareness. It can be useful to think of your psyche as having an attic, a main floor, and a basement. We spend most of our time on the main floor, which has a kitchen, bathroom, bedroom, and living area. We don't *need* to go anywhere else if we don't want to. However, containing and expressing the maximum amount of spiritual energy requires you to explore and even feel comfortable roaming around all three floors of your psyche's layout.

Let's take a walk downstairs to your basement. You might want to close your eyes and get a picture or feeling of what is down there. It may be dark and have stuff piled in all the corners. On the other hand, it may be well lit and relatively free of clutter—I doubt it though. You see, the basement of your psyche is where you store everything that you don't want to look at or feel. This would be a fine place to store all those "useless" memories, except for the fact that it takes a tremendous amount of energy to do so. In fact, each piece of stored junk is energy—either in the form of a thought or a feeling. These bits of energy want to move through you just as all of life seeks to extend itself, only every time it starts to float upward toward the main floor, or your conscious awareness, you pile something on top of it to keep it down. Maybe ice cream, or possibly some chaos at work or in a relationship will keep it down for a while longer. Face it: It's exhausting trying to keep the contents of your basement buried.

I once had a dream that I was sitting in the living room of my house, and some scary, ugly people were trying to come up from a hole in the floor. I was literally sitting on a piece of wood covering the hole trying to keep them down when they screamed, "We are going to burn this entire house down if you don't let us out of here!" At that point, I moved out of the way and let them come out—not a pretty sight; as they came up from the basement they were deformed and disheveled. They simply walked past me as if I were irrelevant. It was good; they left, and I still had my house…

Who is living in your basement? Your dreams will tell you (as will your projections). Every aspect of any given dream is said to be a piece of your psyche. If you dream that a promiscuous dancer is trying to seduce your husband, you likely have promiscuous dancer in your basement that, due to her overwhelming power and energy, you banished years ago.

You can gently let them come up, they won't hurt you. They are more dangerous in the basement than in your awareness. These emotional monsters grow in power and strength when we hide and feed them to keep them at bay.

Energy Tip: Keep a dream journal so that you can pay attention to emerging themes. Similar feelings with different characters indicate that an emotional constellation is attempting to break up and move through you.

Your higher self lives in the upper level of your house. This is the part of you that is wise, calm, and joyful. We reach her in meditation or in times of stillness or bliss. You will notice that when you make contact with your higher self, you become infused with pure, positive energy.

The idea is to become aware of and integrate all three levels of your psyche. The power and energy that you experience when you have nothing to hide is beyond description. Insights pour into your mind, joy bubbles up from your belly, and energy flows freely through the unobstructed corridors of your being. All it takes is a willingness to see and feel what you have denied or suppressed. If you'd like, ask your subconscious to clean out your basement slowly through time so that it doesn't become overwhelming. Once you commit to this process, sit back and watch situations and dreams unfold to assist you.

Gut Feelings

For many people, feelings are a primary source of intuition. You walk into a room and immediately feel uncomfortable, or you meet someone and your energy starts dancing in their presence. The feelings in your body provide you with an immense amount of information if heeded. The challenge lies in paying attention to your gut feelings, the subtle physical cues that tend to reside just below the surface of your awareness, and then trusting them enough to honor what they are telling you.

A woman called me this past week to see about getting her daughter in for some counseling and coaching. My body was reacting negatively as I listened to the voice mail. My mind, however, was saying that I "should" take her because I love helping teenagers navigate through this precarious stage in life. As I checked in with my feelings I got the impression that the mother was the problem, and that I wouldn't be able to help. The mother seemed to be denying her own anger while tagging her daughter with "anger management problems." It is common for parents to project their repressed emotions or unlived dreams onto their children, putting the kids in a terrible bind. Kids often don't have the tools to see it for what it is, and therefore accept the picture that's being unfairly projected onto them.

I decided to honor my feelings and told the woman that it wasn't a good fit, and encouraged her to contact another counselor who might be better suited for the situation. The woman became agitated and challenged me on my decision. As I hung up the phone, my body felt light, and I had a sense of relief that I made the right decision. In fact, my intuitive impression of anger in the mother was confirmed during the phone call. Had I ignored the tightness in my belly and went with my more rational thought process, it would have likely turned out to be a waste of time and energy for everyone involved.

Each of us has a built-in radar system to help us navigate through life. In Western society, however, we tend to value the rational mind, often at the expense of our intuition. It takes practice to become skilled at interpreting the various feelings in your body. Each person's response system is unique. The challenge is that most of the time you don't have data to support your gut feelings, at least not initially. Frequently you will find out later that you made a good decision. The life in your body is connected to all of life—at the level of spirit, we are one.

This web of life carries information to which your individual brain doesn't have access.

Energy Tip: Gently tune into to your subtle radar system to guide you through traffic today. Notice if the route you choose saves time and energy!

Occasionally you will have a strong physical reaction caused by something in your immediate environment triggering a traumatic memory in your past. This can be confusing because it is unclear if your strong feelings are intuition or traumatic flashback.

These "flashbacks" are normal in that everyone experiences either emotional or physical trauma at some point in life. Your task is to become aware of the traumatic energy pockets in your system so that you can manage them and support the clearing process instead of reacting to them as if they were intuitive information.

Suppose you were in a car accident many years ago, and now every time you approach the intersection where the accident took place you feel panicky. We often block out sources of anxiety and forget details. Therefore, it would be easy to attribute your uneasiness to intuition telling you to take another route. However by shining the light of awareness on your body you will likely remember the source of your feelings, freeing you to make the best choice.

The way to distinguish a traumatic memory from intuition is by tuning in to the feelings in your body. Emotional energy from trauma tends to be debilitating. When it comes to the surface, you usually have a response much like a fight-or-flight reaction. Your heart rate increases, the blood rushes from your extremities, and you feel panic. The antidote to this extremely uncomfortable flood of emotion is to breathe and comfort yourself as you would a small child having the same experience. In time, it will pass.

Intuitive information, on the other hand, brings a sense of calm. It is as if you are objectively observing the information rather than the energy taking over your body, as occurs with traumatic flooding.

On occasion you will perceive intuitive information that feels urgent—however, you will still feel calm underneath the impending message. These strong intuitive messages may involve your physical safety, or the feelings may be trying to convey something you have been ignoring. In time, you will be able to discern the difference between intuitive feelings in your body and old emotions that are surfacing.

Don't be afraid to make some mistakes. Learning to use your built-in radar takes practice. It is an invaluable

tool for managing your energy resources—and in addition to being extremely practical, it's a lot of fun!

Chapter 3
Organize Your Thoughts

Research on the mind/body connection is expanding the way we look at intelligence. Although the brain clearly orchestrates much of what goes on in the body, there is evidence that each of our cells contain inherent intelligence as well. Despite this expanded view of the mind, many of us continue to direct the vast majority of our attention toward our brains, causing an overall energy imbalance.

If a machine were to scan your body to see the distribution of energy, it would likely pick up a strong concentration above your shoulders. Many of us over-identify with the mundane thoughts swimming around in our heads at the expense of our bodies. It seems that we have figured out how to suck serotonin and other chemicals out of our brains at will to get a short-term energy boost.

This manipulation of one's body chemistry and pre-occupation with repetitive thinking has resulted in what may be the biggest addiction we face: addiction to ob-session. Excessive energy directed toward one's brain gives it too much power, creating a self-defeating energy pattern that needs to be reversed.

Your energy source is located closer to the center of your body. We also get energy from the environment through proper breathing and an organic dance of give and take. Squeezing energy out of your brain is parallel to the high that comes from a spontaneous shopping spree. You may get a short burst, but you will pay the price later.

The following is a list of the topics explored in this section. Here we are reminded that for maximum bright-ness we need to put the brain in its proper place, ensur-ing that it supports overall self-expression. This involves disciplining your thoughts so that they do not sabotage your efforts, as well as redistributing the energy through-out your entire mind/body. When this is accomplished, every part of you works together harmoniously.

- Awareness
- Silence
- Directing Your Energy
- Assessing Versus Judging

- ৵ Affirmations
- ৵ Perception
- ৵ Intuitive Thoughts

Awareness

All addictions require a lack of awareness to survive. Any time you shine the light of awareness onto a compulsive ritual, the resulting gratification—even if misguided—disappears. The payoff seems to come from the surge of energy received when initiating a compulsive ritual—only there is always a subsequent lull.

For many of us, obsessive thinking is a ritual. Your attention moves up toward your head and you begin to go in circles like a merry-go-round at the fair. Other than providing a false sense of security and control, this circular thinking gets us nowhere. Furthermore, every time you jump on this mental merry-go-round you feed the ritual vital energy, causing the habit to become more entrenched in your psyche.

The attention and energy directed toward obsessive thinking fuels the ritual that then provides us with a boost whenever we decide that a "fix" is needed. Do you see the craziness of it all? We give energy and attention from our unlimited supply to a pattern that then gives us back a limited supply on demand... It is self-deception at its best.

Why not simply rely on the unlimited, fully nourishing supply at hand? It all comes down to a need for control. You may as well stand there with your hands on your hips saying, "I will decide where, when, and how I get my energy—*now leave me alone!*" The idea of putting your thoughts in their proper place—a tool to support authentic self-expression—can back your ego into a corner and cause it to play literal mind games with you. In his book *A New Earth*, Eckhart Tolle says, "Ego is no more than this: identification with form, which primarily means thought forms."

Loosening the grip of your frightened and often obsessive ego is a process that needs to be approached lightly. Awareness is key. You can begin by making time each day to become aware of your spiritual nature (the life that is in you and moves through you). An awareness of your spiritual core creates a gentle shift in identification from the limited ego—repetitive thoughts—to the vastness of who you are. Once you *know* that you are more than your thoughts, body, and personality, it is less threatening to surrender control to the flow of life.

Breathing with awareness helps to shine a light on unconscious thought patterns. Mindful breathing from your diaphragm actually redistributes the energy in your body so that it is not so concentrated in your head.

You can also start to pay attention to the quality of your thoughts. The main reason unproductive thoughts have so much power is because we simultaneously feed them energy while ultimately ignoring their content—an extremely efficient way to create a monster. Paying attention to what you're really thinking will leave you scratching your head asking why you are torturing yourself with such nonsense.

Energy Tip: Make a point to frequently follow your breath, allowing your attention to "drop down" into your body. This redistribution of energy will at once lessen the grip of the ego and strengthen your identification with your spiritual nature.

When too much of your energy is tied up in repetitive and unproductive thinking, the one inner point of reference that seeks to guide you to your highest level of fulfillment is often ignored. As awareness expands, you will increasingly sense the will of life.

Make a commitment to be aware of your thoughts—only then can you gain back the control you have lost and thereby *choose* what you will, and won't, entertain in that brilliant mind of yours.

Silence

Silence is beyond golden; it is platinum.

One of the most common questions asked of me as an energy coach is how to quiet the mind. Silence in your mind provides so much benefit that once you experience even a fraction of the resulting bliss, you will be hooked.

Quieting your thoughts is like playing golf: If you try to force it, it will backfire. Cultivating mental silence requires an indirect approach. As you know, you can't instruct your brain to stop thinking. Resulting thoughts would likely be, "Stop thinking about what...I need to eat...what do I have in the kitchen...leftover ravioli from last night sounds good...Oh yeah, stop thinking...*stop thinking*!" Rather, you might sneak through the basement by focusing on your breath and your body, waiting for the beloved instant of stillness to emerge.

These platinum moments of stillness bring with them incredible amounts of pure, fresh, core energy. In only an instant of mental silence you will feel energy exploding in every cell of your body and brain simultaneously. Not only does this infusion leave you brilliantly energized, but it also clears your thoughts leaving you feeling as though your brain has been reformatted, creating space for completely new material.

A daily dose of mental stillness is one of the most proactive things you can do to keep yourself energized and on purpose. I recommend tying it into your morning charging ritual by simply intending to have at least a moment or two of mental silence. Sometimes you will have much more—but if you start with the goal of an instant, you will not get discouraged and give up. And you *will* notice the benefits of even one instant. Life moves through us naturally—it is how we are built. Our job is to support, rather than impede, the flow of life, by remaining clear. Cultivating emotional, mental, and physical clarity is how we support self-expression or the flow of life. Moments of silence plant the seeds for mental clarity.

Another way to achieve stillness is to spend time in nature. It is as if the inherent stillness in nature has the effect of expanding one's energy to the point of relieving pressure in the brain, allowing it to rest. Something about the "beingness" of big trees and fresh air helps us remember to Be.

Energy Tip: When circular thoughts are making you crazy, put your awareness on your big toe. Within seconds you will notice your shoulders drop as the energy moves down your body.

Intellectual competence is a gift that I'm not intending to minimize. Our thoughts simply need to be consciously directed and balanced with periods of rest. Taking time out from thinking helps keep energy evenly distributed throughout the body, and supports the appropriate function of the brain. Putting your brain in charge of your spirit is like making your child head of the household. It is simply not the appropriate hierarchy.

As your awareness expands beyond your brain, providing much-needed moments of stillness, it becomes free to fulfill its natural function of supporting your inner light to shine.

Directing Your Energy

Your thoughts have the power to either expand or limit the amount of energy moving through your system. Many of us are so identified with our thoughts that we forget that we have the power to direct them in a way that affects our quality of life. The first step is to assess our thoughts objectively regarding how they are, or *are not*, supporting self-expression.

Some statistics state that we use a mere 7 percent of our brains. Regardless of the exact percentage, research shows that we use only a small portion of our total mental capacity. In addition to operating way below our potential, we tend to think the same thoughts over and over. Limited and repetitive thinking yields a limited and repetitive life. These habitual thoughts can be pictured as grooves in the brain that get deeper each time your awareness goes down this mindless path, the way an ice skater would traverse a figure eight.

These mental grooves create templates through which we direct our life energy.

It might be useful to picture yourself with your spiritual energy coming from your abdomen and moving upward toward self expression. As it gets to your heart area, you begin to feel your emotions, which flow along the current of life. Finally, the life energy moves through your brain where it gets shaped by your thoughts. This energy, infused with emotion and shaped by your thought forms, then moves beyond you and into the environment as self-expression. Expansive expression provides abundant energy to you and the world.

Limited thinking constricts the flow of energy in two ways. First, energy flows in the direction of our thoughts, but repetitive thoughts create a small and narrowly defined passageway for expression. Second, what we think about affects our emotional expression. For example, when you view a particular situation as hopeless, you resist life, causing emotions to become heavy and stagnant, thereby impeding energy flow. Bottom line: expanding your awareness beyond familiar thought patterns has a tremendous affect on the quality of your self-expression.

Great thinkers have learned how to cultivate an expansive state of mind. I am quite certain that Einstein did not come upon the theory of relativity through repetitive thinking. For the past 20 or more years, my own brilliant father has been pondering what he calls the ULE or universal logical expression. He defines the ULE, as the most basic law of existence, on which all other principles are built. Whenever he begins to reflect upon this vast concept, he expands his awareness until it is well outside the confines of his own mind. You might say that he rises above his thoughts, in a state of receptivity in which he is able to perceive pieces of the puzzle that are beyond his familiar thinking. He believes that there is no way for him to get insights of this magnitude while remaining a "fish in a fishbowl."

Have you ever found yourself listening to a loved one with a completely open mind, only to be flooded with compassion and understanding? It is amazing what we see when we can expand our awareness beyond the familiar mental grooves.

Regular meditation has the effect of expanding one's mental awareness. You can also engage in daily mental workouts. Simply choose to deliberately keep your mind open and expansive for a certain amount of time—say a half hour—and notice how much more you perceive, as well as how much better you feel!

Energy Tip: Whenever you find that you're in a foul mood, notice what you are thinking about, and then release it. Tell yourself that it is not necessary to know all the answers. Watch your awareness expand and your mood lighten.

It is easier to cultivate mental discipline when you expand your identification beyond familiar thoughts. This involves cultivating the ability to observe your thoughts. The observer position is a powerful one in which you align with your higher self while watching your thoughts. For most of us, this provides a much-needed break. The creative energy necessary to facilitate real change in our lives can only come from temporarily detaching from old ways of thinking long enough to allow life to flow in and loosen the mental patterns a bit.

Repetitive thoughts do provide a security blanket of sorts. They feel safe because they are familiar. When we stay in the same thought patterns we know what to expect—how we will feel and what we will perceive. Everything goes through the same old lens. Perhaps we can have some compassion for ourselves as we desperately hold on to familiar thoughts in this rapidly changing and sometimes scary world.

As you expand your mind, you create more space for life to move. Just as a stream feeds the surrounding landscape as it flows, you too will feel more charged and nourished when your essence flows expansively through your mind.

Assessing Versus Judging

Energy travels more lightly when it is not laden with heavy emotional judgments. When we keep in mind the goal of supporting authentic self-expression, judging another becomes a burden not worth carrying.

Once again, our egos have tricked us into believing that judging puts us in a superior position. Energetically speaking, this is impossible. So what is it about judging that makes it so easy to fall into? Why do we do it at all? The truth is that we are not doing it, our egos are.

Your higher self would no more judge your neighbor than it would itself. It's not that this doesn't happen—we are often our own harshest critic. Judging appears to be a ploy to keep us on top, but it actually serves to keep the ego in charge. The only control our egos have is whether to support or resist energy flow. But we have managed to construct some pretty amazing tactics to convince ourselves that we are in control of the river of life.

The difference between assessing and judging resides in the emotional content of the thought. Assessing involves making light and flexible observations. In other words, when the picture shifts, so does your perception. There is no *attachment* to assessments.

Judging, on the other hand, has a heavier emotional quality. Because of the energy invested in the judgment, we become attached to it—a good or bad label gets slapped onto the perception, and then it is locked into place. Then, as if it were one of our babies, we hold on to it for dear life.

Because of their restrictive nature, judgmental thoughts lower our energy and therefore feed the parts of us that are of a similar quality or vibration. For this reason, you may experience some "withdrawals" when you stop judging. You may crave a good gossip session or an excuse to put people in their places as the other low energy forms start to dissipate. In the absence of heavy judgments, the lower energy will transmute and become lighter. At some point you will no longer experience an energy payoff from being judgmental. In fact, it will bring you down and leave you feeling a little poisoned.

Energy Tip: Notice how you feel when you judge. Perhaps you're feeding yourself the equivalent of junk food. Try to purify your thoughts and see if you feel more like you've eaten a fresh apple.

I'm sure you've noticed that when you observe or assess a situation rather than judge it, your perception improves. This is because retaining an open mind allows us to readily accommodate changes in our perceptions.

When assessing, you'll also notice that you have less of a need to share your observations because you are not attached to them being fixed. You no longer need another's approval that you are "right."

Assessing frees both you and the person or situation you're observing. When we look at someone through judgmental eyes, we cast an energy mold upon them that they can feel. It makes it more difficult for them to gracefully move into healthier behavior. If the person is conscious and aware, he will simply cast off your judgments and keep moving. However, if she is young or unconscious, it will be more difficult to break free.

A client recently told me that her son pleaded with her to stop viewing him as troubled. He said that it makes it hard for him to reach his potential when everyone around him views him as a "loser." How beautiful that someone so young was able to articulate such a profound concept.

Judgmental thoughts put limits upon your mind and ultimately block your ability to feel your own essence. They might make you feel secure for a time, but in truth, each judgment adds another bar to an internal prison that you are constructing.

The only way to break free of judgmental constructs is to bring our awareness into the present moment. Judging is simply a habit of thinking. Changing your mind in the present is the key to cultivating mental freedom now and in the future.

Affirmations

It used to be that whenever I thought about affirmations, I would laugh as I remembered the *Saturday Night Live* episode in which Stuart Smalley had Michael Jordan say, "I'm good enough, I'm smart enough, and doggone-it, people like me!" Jordan himself couldn't do the skit without a smirk on his face. The writers of the show were poking fun at a growing number of people catching on to the power of affirmative thinking.

These days, when people ask me if affirmations really work, I tell them that they changed my life. As a student of *A Course in Miracles* (a spiritual self-study book, published by Foundation for Inner Peace, consisting of 365 affirmations to be done throughout the year), I went from being a fragile, somewhat neurotic young woman, to a resilient, strong (and not quite as young) woman.

Repeating statements that reflect the truth, or an aspect of your potential, bring forth the reality that they affirm. This is true whether the statements are negative or positive. Stating the positive truth about yourself and the world brings you in closer alignment with the nature of life. This is true partly because uplifting thoughts are not resistant to but supportive of energy flow, and partly because we *are* fundamentally positive.

Carey tells herself everyday that she hates her job. She gets very specific. She thinks about hating her boss, her clients, her commute, and even a few of her colleagues. Not only does she think about these things daily, but she also tells her mother and her friends. Carey has hated her job for eight years.

Sydney glares at her thighs in the mirror. "I'm so fat," she declares. Every single day she affirms the very reality she is desperate to escape.

Affirmations alone may or may not cause Carey to fall in love with her job, or turn Sydney into a leggy supermodel. What we do know is that, if these women would be willing to replace these thoughts with something more positive, they would each experience a shift in perception (what *A Course in Miracles* defines as a miracle), thereby releasing the thoughts that are keeping them in a state of inner turmoil.

As I write these words I am single and have been for nearly four years. I am in what I consider the prime of my life and would love to share it with someone special. I could easily dwell on my singleness as I watch the man in the office across from me leap off to the beach with his new girlfriend days after separating from his wife, or as I notice the handsome couple sharing an intimate meal at the corner table of Scottsdale's hippest restaurant. I could dwell on the question I asked several times a week am at a minimum: "So…meet a man yet?" Aside from my faith in life and the power it has to attract whatever I need at the right time, my most recent affirmation is, "My life is written in my soul—it wants me as much as I want it." No need to put internal (or external, thank you very much) pressure on myself.

Here are the rules for affirmations:

1. Choose positive wording, such as "I *am* fit," versus "I *am not* fat."

2. State it in the present tense: "I *am*" rather than "I *will be*."

3. Repeat it as often as possible—20 times a day or more.

4. Make sure it is true—at least in potential.

The energy of affirmations has the power to transform you so quickly that you will make Madonna in the 1980s and '90s look stagnant. I recommend starting with the area of your life that bothers you the most. Turn your negative self-talk into a positive affirmation.

Get an intuitive sense of your potential. At this place, you are successful, organized, attractive, and loved. Affirm the truth of your potential until it sinks down into your subconscious mind. Once it gets down there, your work will be done. You will then act "as if"—the surest way to attract that which you desire. Below are some examples of effective affirmations.

- ᕦ Abundance permeates my life.
- ᕦ I am healthy and fit.
- ᕦ I am loved.
- ᕦ I am organized.
- ᕦ My life is paradise.

There are an infinite number of statements that affirm your highest potential. Don't be shy with these. Of course, you won't want to announce them to the world but simply be bold within your self and with your choice of affirmations.

Energy Tip: Choose an area of your life in which you are not satisfied. Note the amount of energy you spend obsessing on it, and vow to replace related thoughts with an affirmation that reflects your potential.

Making a commitment to direct your energy toward what you *do* instead of *don't* want is like repairing a leak in your car's gas tank. Not only will you "run" better, but you will also have more fuel, which is your ultimate source of inner peace and joy.

Perception

We perceive based on the lens through which we are looking. Each of us has multiple lenses. Becoming familiar with your different sets of eyes helps discern the validity of your perceptions. Not only do your internal lenses or thought templates direct energy outward, but they filter what comes in as well.

Say for example you wake up on the wrong side of the bed. You have no clean clothes, your coffee machine decides to break down, and, after navagating to Starbucks, you find that the line is too long and you have to leave empty-handed. As you make your way through rush hour traffic, someone pulls in front of you so close that it puts you inches away from a highway pile-up. You become so angry that you can hardly see straight. Logically, you know that the lens currently filtering your perception is not your highest self, but that doesn't stop you from being in a bad mood all day.

Say you decided to step up your awareness and intervene. You don't necessarily remove the "off to a terrible start" lens; rather, you choose to be aware that you have it on along with the implications of continuing to look through that particular lens. There is nothing wrong with choosing to stay grumpy for a little while—you may even catch your higher self having a chuckle or two at your behavior—met your very awareness begins to lighten your mood.

I teach interpersonal communication. Every semester a group of fresh-faced college students eagerly absorb the principles they will use for a lifetime. One concept at which many of them marvel is the power of their perceptions to deceive them into seeing, hearing, and sensing what they expect, rather than what is real.

To illustrate this point on a basic level, I write a statement shown to me years ago on the board and ask several students to read it out loud.

Seattle in the
the Springtime

Once, all 25 students read it out loud, and not one of them saw the extra "the." You may or may not have seen it. If you did see it, congratulations, you have a very open mind. If you did not see it, congratulations, you have developed efficient perception.

It truly is a double-edged sword—we have to be adept at taking in what we want and filtering out what we don't want. There is way too much going on around us to take in everything—we would literally go crazy.

However, make no mistake about it, you see what you expect to see, hear what you expect to hear, and often feel your own suppressed emotions while assuming they are coming from someone else.

Clear perception is possible, and liberating. I'm sure you have experienced it many times. It is what happens when you are free of internal distractions and sincerely wishing to understand the person or situation in front of you. No emotional baggage involved, no attachment to the outcome, no judgment to muddy the waters. Simply an open, clear observation—this is when you can really see, and it's lovely.

Part of reclaiming your energy involves increasing awareness of when internal debris is clouding your lens and therefore being projected outward. These projections are a combination of emotional energy and mental constructs. They block your expression—plain and simple. They are not useful, and can be harmful. Can we get rid of them completely? Maybe—surely for moments at a time—but we can certainly become aware of them and how they influence pure self-expression and communication with another.

Energy Tip: If you feel depleted—check your lens. It may be cracked, or filthy and in need of a good cleaning.

I can't stress enough how much an open mind supports the flow of energy. The layers upon layers of judgments that we entertain certainly provide a security of sorts. Even shedding a few of the top layers increases mental transparency through which life can flow. We all strive to be beautifully bright from within. We need only to remind ourselves that pure life energy expressed through each layer of our beings will provide the kind of charging that yields overflowing life.

Intuitive Thoughts

Clearing your mind of unwanted assumptions, beliefs, and judgments makes room for the very special gift of clear thinking or mental intuition. It is simply your natural ability to receive and perceive information contained in the life that is flowing through your being.

If you are cerebral—the type of person that has a sharp and quick mind—you may find that cleaning house upstairs provides more benefits than you ever imagined.

Because we are all connected at the level of spirit, your essence contains information to which your brain does not have access. Mental intuition is your natural ability to discern information at a very high level. Imagine you are flying in an airplane above the city where you live. Out your window you can see a bigger picture than when driving down the street. From this level imagine also that you can see what streets are free for drivers, who is sad, who is desperately afraid, and what effect your choices would have on the whole.

Intuition provides this view. Using your intuition to make decisions guarantees two things. First, that you are doing what is best for the whole of you. And second, that your choices serve the whole of humanity. The reason I stress this is because so many people have difficulty making decisions they perceive as "selfish." Your spiritual self will often urge you to take care of yourself in a given situation while your socialized self might feel it is "right" to take care of another.

Your thoughts are one way to receive messages from a higher perspective. Mental intuition is abundant when our minds are clear of repetitive and obsessive thoughts. You may already be aware of the difference between intuitive thoughts and circular thinking. You'll find that intuitive thoughts are often inspiring and complete, filling you with conviction that they are right. This way of receiving information is so natural that it is easy to dismiss the flashes of information that seem to appear out of nowhere.

All we really need to do to cultivate this channel of intuition is to develop mental discipline so that our minds aren't behaving as untrained dogs, jumping up and barking all the time. Energy will rush into a clear mind, providing nourishment and information. As you perceive information contained in the energy, notice how it is different from your thoughts, and how it feels clean and free of erroneous facts. We feel lighter and more expansive when life energy is able to reach our brains.

Energy Tip: If you have a headache, go dig in the dirt. The texture of mud on your hands will distract you from your thoughts long enough for the tension to dissipate.

Fritz Pearls, a famous Gestalt therapist used to say, "Get out of your mind and come to your senses." It is a curious thing that the best utilization of our minds occurs when we stop thinking. Many innovative thinkers say that when they get stuck on something, they leave it for a while. Often, the solution will just come to them in the shower or while immersed in something completely unrelated.

Energy flow is the goal. Becoming aware of our thoughts, silencing our minds in daily practice, and excavating judgments and outworn beliefs, all facilitate the process of life moving through us and beyond. The intuitive information received along the way is an added bonus!

Chapter 4

Appreciate Your Body

How do you feel about your body? Do you love your body as your home, or do you despise it for "not cooperating?" There is great pressure to look a certain way in our society. Preoccupation with our bodies is rampant, even going so far as self-loathing. A tree does not reprimand its apples for being oddly shaped; why would we scold our bodies for being unique?

Highly charged individuals have a secret. They know that when they are firmly planted in the ground, getting enough nourishment, and simply being themselves, their apples are lovely.

Your body plays an important role in personal energy management. It is your home, the place in which you receive, contain, and express pure life energy. It can either facilitate or block self-expression—depending upon how you treat it.

I recently learned of a man who is paraplegic. He, along with nearly 40 other men and women, cycled more than 500 miles through the mountains of Utah and Colorado to raise money for a poor village in Mexico. He rode a specially designed bicycle that allowed him to pedal with his arms. My brother-in-law, Kevin, had the privilege of riding with him several times throughout their five-day journey. While riding, the two of them talked extensively about many subjects, including what it's like to live life in a wheelchair. When asked about his view on stem cell research, this man told Kevin that he doesn't follow the research because he's too busy living and enjoying life.

Just like Kevin's new friend, we all have the option of being so comfortable with our bodies that we naturally inspire others. Evaluating how you view your body is the first step to increasing your physical energy capacity. Once you are aware, the sky's the limit.

Reading the sections listed here will give you an opportunity to evaluate the relationship you have with your body and see if it needs your attention.

- ✑ Body Perspective
- ✑ Reclaiming Your Body
- ✑ Beauty
- ✑ Physical Integrity

- ☞ Eating for Peace
- ☞ Shedding Layers
- ☞ Metabolism and Energy

Body Perspective

Before we can increase our capacity to physically contain and express spiritual energy, we need to ensure that we're viewing our bodies in proper perspective. For some, the task is to reclaim the body, while others may need to expand their awareness beyond the body.

The section on staying grounded in Chapter 1 explored how, as a society, we collectively reject our bodies. There is a vein of thought that the physical body is sinful, lustful, and potentially out of control, leading us down a dark path. News flash: Your body follows your thoughts, not the other way around. If our bodies are out of control, it is because our thoughts are undisciplined and spoiled.

If you have disciplined thoughts, take good care of your body, and appreciate it daily, congratulations, for you have transcended the collective "bad body" belief. If you're not there yet, keep reading. Following are some of the ways the "bad body" myth manifests:

- ☞ A subtle feeling that sex is dirty, or,
  alternatively, indulgence in secret
  underground sexual pursuits.

- Extreme focus on spirituality without physical self-care.
- Anger towards your body for not being healthy or fit enough.
- Negative judgments of people who appear "overly" body conscious.

The previous examples are indications of a spirit/matter split. Collectively we are moving toward embodied spirituality, and therefore, maintaining such a split is becoming more and more uncomfortable.

Some of us live out the spirit/matter split in the opposite way—over-identification with the body accompanied by a lack of awareness of the spiritual self. We experience this when we excessively focus on how we look, what we drive, the kind of work we do, and other aspects of the material world.

It is easy to fall into body identification. Media and Western society foster the view that we are primarily physical. The following is a list of some indicators of physical over-identification.

- Thoughts centered primarily on looks, activities, and purchases.
- Weight fluctuations that create obsessive thinking and discomfort.
- Habitual surgeries or invasive procedures used to combat aging or imperfections.

ى Judgments directed at others who physically "fall short."

These beliefs are unconscious and can be best identified by looking at your behavior and the content of your thoughts. If you fall into either of the previous categories—rejection of your body or over-identification with your body—do not beat yourself up for even one second. Most of us fall somewhere on one side or the other, though we are all headed toward integration of spirit and matter.

Energy Tip: Commit to cultivating a relationship with the rejected parts of you. If it is your body, vow to bring it back into your loving awareness. If your spirit has gone temporarily underground—take a few minutes each day to invite it back into your world.

All this said, what is the best way to view our bodies? Simply put: as a means to an end—a beautiful, sacred, unbelievably intelligent means to an end. Our bodies are amazing vessels through which life extends. For some of us, our bodies are the last level of self, after the spiritual, emotional, and mental levels, to become fully charged with energy. For others, the body is first. Many athletes, for example, thrive on the ability to physically contain a lot of energy. And in some cases, physical mastery can lead to an experience of one's spiritual essence. Regardless of whether you are trying to bring your body up to speed on this journey or the other way around, viewing your body in proper perspective is essential.

We put too much pressure on our bodies when we make them responsible for our happiness and success. When we look to them to fulfill us with their taste buds, or require them to look a certain way solely to capture love and adoration from others, we are asking that they supply us with energy.

Seeing your body as a means of authentic self-expression and taking good care of it so that it can fulfill its function as a strong vessel for life gives it the job for which it was intended. This frees your entire energetic system to function optimally. As a byproduct, your body will respond by evolving to its potential.

As mentioned previously, your energy system is composed of the following levels: spiritual, emotional, mental, and physical. Energy is meant to flow from your spiritual core through each of these energy centers and out into the world. Your body is the densest level, and is three times removed from your source. Viewing it as an object to supply your happiness is an outside-in perspective, and always leaves you feeling empty.

Our bodies thrive when freed to physically charge and express life. Any job other than this will compromise performance and produce results that are counterproductive to the natural order of life. Acceptance of your body occurs once you release it from the pressure of providing you with energy and allow it to fulfill its true function of channeling spiritual energy.

Reclaiming Your Body

As many of us do, I have spent years of my life rejecting my body. The imperfections, pockets of extra padding—all of it—faced my ridicule day after day, year after year. One day in the not too distant past, I had an epiphany. In that moment, I knew that if I did not immediately choose to love my body completely—as I would my child—I could potentially extend the madness for another decade or more. This was unthinkable. Four decades of self-rejection extended? Forget it!

As I began to affirm, "I LOVE MY BODY," something miraculous occurred. The very next morning while getting ready to take my daughter to school, I slipped into my jeans and felt something I had never felt—comfortable, even sensual, in my own skin. "Wow," I thought. "This must be what the people who don't despise their bodies feel like!" I was hooked.

I got rid of the first layer of this neurosis many years ago. I hadn't obsessed about what I ate or how much I weighed for more than a decade. This subtle residue of body rejection remained, and even felt normal. The process of bringing energy into each and every cell of our bodies requires more than a lack of obsession—it requires unconditional love.

The reason I suggest loving our bodies as we love our children is because such love is unconditional. We don't require our children to be physically perfect, although often we feel that they are perfect—completely unique and beautiful. We could never reject or judge these little angels for not meeting a specific set of standards. Why in heaven would we judge ourselves?

Body rejection is tragic no matter how fat, skinny, short, tall, bumpy, boney, or rolly you might be. Consider this: Have you ever seen a child thrive in a harsh and judgmental environment? They cannot. In fact, research on human development shows that healthy attachments (energy connection rather than rejection) are essential for growth—physically, mentally, emotionally, and spiritually.

Judgments block connection. Judgments block life. Therefore, if you are judging your body, you are blocking the creative life energy needed for it to transform! We think we will love our bodies once they behave and do what we want them to do, but it is impossible for them to move, change, grow, or transform unless we love them *as they are.*

Energy Tip: Pick an aspect of your body that you appreciate and be grateful for it every day. Notice how the positive attention expands, moving toward more love and appreciation of your entire body.

Any rejected part of you costs you. It takes more energy than you can imagine to bury the disapproved-of pieces of yourself. Further, it leaves you a partial person.

I recently read an excerpt from Carole Radziwill's memoir, *What Remains* (Scribner, 2005), about the loss of her husband, Anthony Radziwill, and dear friends John F. Kennedy, Jr., and Carolyn Bessette Kennedy. She shared that her first impression of John Kennedy was "entirety." "He is complete in a way that I've never seen," says Radziwill.

Granted, it is a stretch for nearly anyone to compare themselves to John F. Kennedy, Jr.; however, I believe that we can each attain "entirety." Entirety implies a rare and evolved level of self-acceptance—a level that those of us who are called to usher in the next wave of brightness need to attain.

"Perfection not required," could be stamped on the guidebook used to help us relax into our entirety. The only requirement is commitment. With determination, body love is attainable. Look down right now at your most sweetly obnoxious love handle or stretch mark and commit to embracing it as a piece of the art that is you.

Beauty

As the saying goes, beauty is as beauty does. Studies may be able to define objective beauty by a certain set of features, but true and enduring beauty is more about the light shining through your eyes and skin.

Have you ever seen someone classically beautiful or handsome, only to have that fade as you got to know him? What about the opposite—nothing special at first, but then after a short time she seems really attractive?

Everyone, and I mean everyone, has the capacity to be tremendously beautiful, and should not settle for anything less. Beauty is an inherent attribute of spiritual energy, and therefore, *everyone* who is spiritually charged is beautiful. There are three steps to cultivating your inherent beauty. The first is to make a commitment to stop comparing yourself to external standards as defined by society and media. Next you commit to unabashed self-expression. Finally you engage in a full-on love affair—with yourself.

Stop Comparing

It is challenging to look at a magazine and not instantly think of a long list of things about yourself that you would change if you could. We are bombarded with images of beauty that fit into a narrowly defined set of parameters that describe a mere fraction of the population. The models portrayed in the glossy airbrushed photos are stunning and certainly beautiful even when they are not airbrushed. But so are you. The only difference between these models and the rest of us is that their beauty is acknowledged and celebrated. Despite the image we project onto them, my hunch is that even these "perfect" beauties compare themselves to their thinner, taller, or more voluptuous counterparts, engaging in the futile and all-too-common habit of self-judgment.

We could all do with a little more compassion toward ourselves, and a lot less comparing. Comparing yourself to someone else is like a daisy comparing itself to a sunflower. Both are beautiful in their own right. It would be so sad if all flowers except sunflowers wilted in discouragement that they were not taller and brighter. Yet flowers don't have brains that construct ideal images. They simply express life fully through their unique form—huh, I think they're on to something...

Unabashed Self-Expression

The other day I met a friend after work at a wine bar for a visit and a glass of pinot. It must have been one of those days, because I, myself, felt a little wilted. My friend is tall, dark-eyed, and European—you get the picture. As a coach and aspirant of complete self-love, I gave myself a pep talk. "It's okay Kim, we are all different, just be yourself...." Then it occurred to me that all I really needed to do was to be open and loving (thank you, God—I love these insights).

I arrived about 10 minutes before my friend with an open heart and wide eyes. As I stood looking around for a place to sit, I noticed someone looking at me and smiling. I smiled back, of course.

I found a seat and struck up a conversation with the gentleman next to me who was getting ready to start his own lobbying firm. My friend arrived in the midst of our conversation, stunning as always. I was unaffected.

After we got our table I maintained my openness. My back was to the crowd and I was positioned in a place where I could only see my friend. My energy must have still been flowing strongly, however, because people kept talking to me. At one point, a woman walked by, touched my shoulder and said, "Can you believe how crowded it is tonight?" My friend, who tends to like my full attention, gestured to the whole place and said, "She's with me, alright?!" And then to me, "Why does everyone keep talking to you?" She then proceeded to tell the rest of her story as I smiled inside, practicing what I preach: authentic, heart-based, self-expression.

Fall in Love

Okay, I'm the first to acknowledge that it sounds syrupy, but falling in love with yourself is mandatory if you want to achieve blinding brightness. I prescribe a "self-love campaign" to nearly every one of my clients. A few have it down, and I congratulate them wholeheartedly.

There are many stories of famous people advised to have plastic surgery or to lose weight in order to fill an external mold or standard. Those who refuse are heroic in my opinion—embracing themselves fully. Invariably, the feature they were asked to "fix" becomes their trademark. When we accept and love ourselves, others accept and love us as well. People can sense when you reject a part of yourself, and they tend to reject it as well, which you become aware of, on and on. Voila! A self-fulfilling prophecy.

Falling in love with *you* requires mental discipline. Affirming your potential is always a good idea: "I am fit and healthy," or "my ethnicity is exotic." You can transform any part of yourself that you dislike simply by changing how you think about it. In fact, you can change your behavior by changing your thoughts. If, for instance, you want to lose weight, thinking of yourself as healthy will cause you to make healthy choices.

People get confused about the concept of discipline. It is 90-percent mental and 10-percent physical. If you train your mind, your body will follow. Of course, there are times when you have to physically make yourself exercise, or not eat that second bowl of ice cream, or whatever, but true discipline is the result of paying careful attention to your thoughts.

When you completely accept yourself, you open up on the inside and make more room for energy to move through you, which is the source of all happiness and joy. So go for it—be yourself, express yourself, and love yourself!

Physical Integrity

Spiritual energy is intense. Expressing it at a high velocity requires your vessel or container to be solid, flexible, and free of excess debris—the very definition of physical integrity. When we plug in to our internal source, the flowing energy loosens and clears away emotional and physical congestion. The natural intensity of spiritual energy combined with this decongestion process can be overwhelming to the point of making you feel a desperate need to calm it down, or to numb out.

Enter ice cream. There is no better way to calm intense energy than cool, creamy ice cream. Ah...relief sets in as you take bite after bite of Cherry Garcia. Finally, you are finished—in fact, the pint is empty. Officially "numbed out," you pick up the remote to do some channel surfing, looking for something to lose yourself in for a while.

If it didn't work, we wouldn't do it. The payoff is immediate. The cost? Well, that's another story. It's a lessened ability to contain your own energy—a diminished capacity if you will. Is this the result of consuming that harmless pint of your favorite ice cream? Eating ice cream is not the problem. It's the way it's eaten that is potentially self-defeating. Each time we consume anything in such a way as to put a lid on our own intensity, stress, or worries, we put holes in our container, becoming more fragile than strong, more porous than solid.

The way to differentiate between a pleasurable treat and a compulsive binge—whether it's food, alcohol, sex, shopping, or any number of activities—is by assessing your mood while you indulge. Are you behaving more like a French woman, slowly enjoying every bite, or acting like a wild animal? Wild animals consume in a frenzy of desperation. And by definition, compulsive consumption is mindless. We go into a place where we disconnect from our breath and awareness in order to suck some energy out of the chosen ritual. Perhaps we just check out and go into autopilot, not tasting anything at all.

If you feel imprisoned by a self-defeating habit or ritual, mindless consuming can serve to keep a dense pocket of emotional energy buried inside you. When thoughtless consuming is used to "stuff feelings," it actually feeds whatever is suppressed that has a similarly dense or low-energy vibration. That is why, when you don't allow yourself to engage in these self-defeating rituals, you get intense cravings. The dense or lower energies in you (unrefined addictive patterns that take on a life of their own) are screaming to be fed. As with pockets of suppressed emotional energy, each time you choose not to feed these pockets of physical congestion they transmute—the internal heat generated from the tension of *not* giving into a craving transforms them into a more refined energy that you can metabolize and release. You will immediately feel the additional life moving through the cleared space. You'll feel empowered.

Whether clearing emotional or physical congestion, the path to freedom is the same: Delay binges of any kind, and when you do partake, do it mindfully.

Giving into a compulsive binge creates holes in your system (container) so that external energy can be brought in immediately. These holes undermine your integrity, impairing your ability to contain and express your own core energy.

Energy Tip: The next time your inner monsters scream at you to feed them, stay in the discomfort and tension for five to 10 minutes while the energy heats up the fire of transformation. Then proceed with awareness. You may find you no longer "need" that which you were seeking.

Some who have dedicated their lives to spirituality find that they require less food and sleep (listen to your intuition on this one—often our bodies require more sleep to support the clearing process) than they previously needed. This is because they have cultivated the ability to metabolize spiritual energy and use it for fuel. And when they do eat, they stay connected to their spiritual core through mindfulness, not over-identifying with the object of consumption. "Cheap" foods (highly processed/low energy content foods) or mindless consumption becomes a downer and is no longer desirable.

Bottom line: delay binges and consume mindfully—through time, it will seal the holes in your container and refine dense, suppressed energies, allowing you to receive, contain, and express your own spiritual essence. Finally, we get real nourishment.

Eating for Peace

There are so many prescriptions for eating right that ultimately, if you researched each and every one of them, you would end up with a huge pile of contradictory information. There is a source, however, that will provide you with specific, tailored information that will lead you to perfect health and balance, and that source is *you*.

Your internal point of reference has likely already informed you of several things that you should be either doing or not doing to promote increased health and balance in your body. It is easy to ignore your inner voice, because it often urges change. Excessive focus on the multitude of external options is one way to avoid doing what you really need to do.

We need to shift our attention inward for relevant guidance. Books and health experts do offer valuable information; however, you will not know if any given piece of advice applies to you unless you get that feeling of resonance. "Ah, that feels right for me!"

Each of us is composed of many facets or layers of uniqueness. These include genetics, followed by environmental factors, followed by years of habits, both good and bad, followed by stage of life, followed by what kind of day you've had... As we make choices dictated by the desire for life to freely and abundantly move through us, we experience inner peace and well-being, which feeds on itself (pardon the pun). Bright Ones are "hooked" on inner peace and naturally make choices that perpetuate well-being.

One's physical potential evolves naturally out of this frame of reference: Energy flows through an open vessel, free of inner congestion (both physical and emotional). The more spiritual energy flowing through you, the more alive and at peace you feel. Therefore, your task prior to eating is to tune into your internal point of reference and ask, "Will this give me inner peace?" I do not mean immediate gratification, but real inner peace in an hour, a day, or a week. When we listen to ourselves and act accordingly, we not only experience inner peace, but also physical health and balance.

The feedback system of inner peace and physical well-being versus inner turmoil and lack of balance provides you with perfect moment-by-moment direction. You know how you're doing based on how you feel. If you're feeling off balance, you can backtrack. You may find yourself thinking about the extra glass of wine you had with dinner the night before, or your restless night's sleep. You may feel sluggish due to lack of exercise. On the other hand, once you make the choices that lead to peace, you won't want to give it up. Feeling good leads to asking, "What do I need to continue to feel this way?"

Energy Tip: Begin to view your body from a place of abundance rather than one of lack. Instead of focusing on what you shouldn't have, vow to *give* yourself something nourishing every day. Some days it might be a walk, or some fresh strawberries—other times it might be an afternoon nap.

Putting your attention on providing your body what it needs instead of taking away what it doesn't creates a synergy of partnership between your mind and your body. For many of us there has been anything but mind/body collaboration. This idea may need to be reintroduced. Give your body praise. If you can walk, you are blessed. If you have been judging your body, consciously forgive and apologize for being so harsh. Actually put your hands on areas that you have mentally rejected in the past and deliberately direct loving energy and acceptance to that area. Your body is intelligent and receptive to love. It will respond with vibrancy and increased willingness to move toward wellness.

Your needs will vary each moment. To adopt programs without the guidance of your intuition is inherently deficient and cannot lead you to your potential. Even if a particular program is right for you at a certain point, your needs will likely evolve depending upon life stages and circumstances.

If you are aware that you need to make a change, but cannot muster up the inner resources to do so, ask yourself what else is going on that you are attempting to escape or buffer yourself from. Once, a client told me that she experienced a direct correlation between lack of sex and increased ice cream consumption... Your internal point of reference will guide you to the source of your imbalance, whether spiritual, emotional, mental, or physical.

Addiction to guilt is another reason that many people stay stuck in bad habits. Hear this: Guilt is like glue. Feelings of guilt keep self-defeating patterns in place and locked in. It's normal, and even healthy, to feel guilty if you steal your mother's retirement money or do behave in some hurtful or slimy way. Even then, it is there to point you in another direction, not for you to settle in and live there! I've met too many people that have guilt as their best friend. They do something that they are not proud of and slip right into guilt/shame mode as a way to punish themselves.

If you experience habitual guilt, then that pattern is the first one that needs to go. All you do is swear off guilt. If you make a bad eating choice, just acknowledge it and move on. Great athletes know this. Do you think Michael Jordan wallowed in guilt every time he missed a shot? He would not have been the performer that he was if he allowed himself to get stuck in that sticky, low-level emotion.

Attention is directed energy, and energy feeds patterns and makes them grow. Eating for peace means placing your attention on what gives you a sense of well-being, and following it like the yellow brick road. You will soon find yourself happy and healthy!

Shedding Layers

People come in all different shapes and sizes. In this way, we mirror nature. There are large flowers and small flowers, enormous mountains and rolling hills. The world is rich and beautiful because of its inherent variety.

Honoring your physical blueprint involves finding the most healthy weight and size for you. Therefore, when I speak of shedding layers, I am not advocating across-the-board thinness. I am suggesting, however, that excess weight beyond one's natural body type contains more than just fat—it carries emotional and physical toxins imprisoned by the weight.

Toxins aren't just contained in fat, however. Many thin people carry emotional and physical congestion in their organs, muscles, and skin, which weighs heavily on their vitality and well-being. Shedding layers is clearing cells. If you have extra weight, that will come off too. Most importantly, your cells will transmute any dense congestion and become clear, increasing your ability to contain more pure life energy.

I've carried an extra 10 pounds or so almost my entire life. In recent years, I have committed to shedding any layers that conceal my radiance, and therefore have released most of what I needed to. Intuitively, I knew it would be good to shed the extra pounds, but never really knew why, and was concerned that it might be a vanity issue. It wasn't until I started letting go of the weight, and accompanying emotional congestion, that I realized my resistance came from wanting to hold on to the security blanket that had become a part of my identity.

When you've held on to layers for a long time, you can be sure that emotional energy is locked inside. This is different from putting on a few pounds during the holidays, or finding yourself weighing a bit more in recent years.

Energy Tip: If you are ready to shed the layers concealing your radiance, commit to a mini-cleanse. Replace a fresh fruit and vegetable juice for one or two meals (total, not daily) each week.

Giving your body a chance to let go of the toxins by eating clean and light, or sticking to juice and soup for a short time, is an extremely efficient way of letting go of old toxins. You may want to start by choosing one or two days a week to "eat clean." This entails forgoing coffee, sugar, soda, and alcohol, and sticking to fresh, light foods—preferably organic.

What works for me is one purification day a week in which I have juice, and then an early dinner of soup or something light. The rest of the week I try to make good choices balanced with my favorite things, along with regular exercise.

I do **not** recommend that people use cleanses or fasting for weight loss—just for purification. Exercise and healthy eating are the way to go. Even if you are thin, purification through a mini-cleanse will release any congestion that you're holding in your cells. Whatever you do, **check with your doctor first**.

Follow your instincts. Once you commit to releasing the layers covering your radiance, your intuition will tell you exactly what to do. You may feel the need to take a break from M&Ms or to cut back on the caramel lattes. Be prepared for a period of detoxification. Its severity will mirror the amount of toxins you are carrying. It is usually short-lived—one to three days—and need only be experienced once if you commit to taking breaks from your favorite things at least once a week. This gives your body a chance to clear out emotional and physical toxins regularly.

The discomfort associated with the shedding of layers is a small price to pay for the lightness of being that results. Along with increased energy and vitality, you will find yourself celebrating inner peace and freedom, and an increased ability to enjoy the present moment. There is nothing like the feeling of spiritual energy flowing freely through your body—the true meaning of "free spirit."

Metabolism and Energy

Being fully charged requires that you not only plug in to your spiritual energy source, but that you hold that charge as well. We are ushering in a new level of integration. Complete spiritual integrity—being charged with energy from your core, embodying it physically, and extending beyond yourself—is sort of like being an organized artist, a creative engineer, or a sexy nun. You embody a level of completeness that is rare. "Spiritual" people are traditionally seen as being more concerned with their inner journey than with physical reality. I believe this is changing, and that evolution is calling us to integrate our spirituality, not only into our thoughts, but also into our bodies.

Consider this paradigm shift: It is as "spiritual" to be physically fit as it is to have a daily spiritual practice. If you are reading these words, it is because you are already charged and desire to keep getting brighter and brighter every day. Your body is not separate from your essence; it is merely an extension. For some of us who have sincerely committed our lives to demonstrating spirituality *in* the world, charging our bodies may be the final phase of total integration, yet it is no less important than clearing our emotions or disciplining our minds.

Being fully energized is intense, and your body needs preparation and training in order to fully contain your powerful essence. An efficient metabolism is the way to increase your physical energy capacity, which is your ability to receive, contain, and express life energy through your body, as well as effectively eat, digest, and eliminate the food you eat. Repairing the holes in your energy system that are created and enlarged each time you compulsively consume is critical to increasing your metabolism and energy capacity. Remember, compulsive consumption is an unconscious attempt to capture immediate energy. It does the trick, but sabotages your energy system, and causes mood swings. The cravings experienced when we delay addictive consumption are symptoms of repair. Just as you have to feel hunger sometimes in order to lose weight, you have to feel short bouts of tension and discomfort in order to seal energy leaks.

We've also discussed the importance of purifying and cleansing the body in order to burn off toxins that build up and clog your body. These toxins affect metabolism, because a large amount of energy is required to compensate for them for the body to function and not get sick. When your body is preoccupied with managing excessive toxins, it can't focus on the important things, like efficient digestion and elimination. An efficient digestive system is a sign of a high metabolism.

Energy Tip: Make sure you have at least one bowel movement a day. If your body is sluggish, buy some aloe vera juice and drink a little before you go to bed. It is a natural and gentle way to aid the elimination process.

Be sure to breathe fully throughout the day as well. Adequate amounts of oxygen aid the body in all its functioning. The idea is to support your body in every way that you can so that it does not have to waste precious energy on clean-up duty. (For more information, see Just Breathe, in Chapter 1.)

Eating only when hungry is also crucial to increasing your metabolism. Hunger is a sign that your body is ready to burn calories. Eating without an appetite is like throwing wood on top of an extinguishing fire—rather than the fiery appetite burning the food and using it as fuel, it simply gets converted to fat.

Exercising regularly and building your muscle mass also increases your ability to metabolize energy. Life has changed. It used to be that people engaged in strenuous physical labor on their farm or in their community. Technology enables most of us to lead fairly sedentary lifestyles.

We need to deliberately exercise our bodies now for them to operate efficiently. For people desiring to lose weight, I recommend focusing on eating for peace and metabolism efficiency rather than watching the scale or stringent dieting. Your body will tell you when it is sluggish and needs activity, or when, for example, it needs more protein or fruit. You will gradually move to your ideal weight with this approach.

Cultivating an efficient metabolism doesn't mean foregoing life's pleasures. What would life be without a stroll in the park, a cocktail or two on a night out, or a few bites of your favorite dessert? Balance is the key. Being bright is first and foremost about love. Giving up what you love is not the answer. The goal is to stop compulsive consumption (which is really just a case of temporary amnesia—you've forgotten where your source lives), and to support your body by taking good care of yourself.

As with all other decisions, your energy and intuition will lead you. At times, the only distance between a bad mood and an overall feeling of well-being is 20 minutes of exercise. Your body will tell you what it wants and needs. This goes for eating the right foods too. My 7-year-old daughter already practices intuitive eating. The other night she wanted some candy from her Halloween basket. I asked her to check in with her stomach—it told her no, but consented to a square of organic dark chocolate from my stash. Imagine if we all learned to tune into our bodies at the age of 7!

Set the intention—tell yourself that you want to be physically efficient (charged with energy, the right weight for you, and fit), and then listen to your body. That's it! Nothing else is required for your essence to permeate your cells and energize your body and extend brightly into the world.

Chapter 5
Assess Your Environment

Although it can be difficult to remember or even believe, your outer world is a direct reflection of your inner world. The external challenges we face always present opportunities to transcend inner patterns that no longer serve us.

The way you relate to others and your environment has a tremendous effect on your energy resources. Do you pour your energy onto people in need? Do you often engage in power struggles with loved ones? Do you manage your time in a way that is nourishing, or depleting?

Not allowing enough time to charge with energy affects your outer world in ways you cannot imagine. In this section, we will look at the relationship between your inner world and your environment. Be prepared to see everything as symbolic—a little objective observation will give you all the information you need to manage your energy in a way that serves you and the world simultaneously.

This chapter includes the following sections:

- Ꭾ Circle of Intimacy
- Ꭾ Forgiveness
- Ꭾ Nourishing Relationships
- Ꭾ Endings
- Ꭾ Work
- Ꭾ Sustainable Living
- Ꭾ Everyday Choices

Circle of Intimacy

For most of us, relationships are among the most important things in life, family and friends usually finding their ways to the top two or three rankings. We are relational beings. Connecting with each other is deeply satisfying and fulfilling.

Sometimes, however, connection leads to pain. Life is bittersweet. I don't think any of us would disagree. We spend a lifetime being raised by our parents, whom we love dearly, and at some point they pass on. Losing a loved one is heartbreaking, but we all know it is part of loving deeply, and most of us wouldn't think of forgoing relationships to avoid the pain of ultimate loss.

There is another type of pain that comes from close relationships. It is the pain of someone hurting you. It may be that one or both of you are neglectful, and that you rarely connect in a meaningful way, or it may be that mean words are exchanged, or other hurtful actions take place.

Here is the truth about energy and relationships: It is very difficult, if not impossible, to receive, contain, and express large amounts of energy in an emotionally unsafe relationship. Chronic emotional pain puts us in a defensive mode in which vital energy is used to build a wall against feelings of pain.

We cannot escape the hurt that comes from emotional insensitivity. It's possible to be numb or frozen while it occurs, but as soon as you thaw out, the pain will attempt to move through you on the natural flow of energy. Principles of energy management direct us to create a safe space to live so that we can open up to energy. This entails looking at the people we let into our inner circles of intimacy.

If you examine your relationships, you will quickly identify those who honor and respect you, and those who do not. Think of the circles of intimacy as concentric circles moving out from your body. Very few people earn their way into your inner circle. Your children and parents (if they are kind), possibly a sibling or a best friend, are usually among the few who get to live in the center of your heart.

Many of us allow people too close when they do not deserve to be there, practically inviting toxins into our energy systems. This robs us of the opportunity to grow brighter each day, because we spend all our valuable resources on self-protection and on processing the multitude of emotional assaults. Some people don't let even the safe people close to their hearts due to a deep-down fear of feeling pain.

Energy Tip: Take the first step of energetic self-care by making a commitment to seeing the truth about your relationships. Simply acknowledging reality, whether painful or not, will bring energy back into your body.

Once we look at our relationships without blinders on, we are empowered to take steps toward creating an energy-friendly environment. Many people ask me, "What if my mother is the one who drains me?" Cultivating a healthy distance from any family member or friend is uncomfortable, but can be done without ending the relationship. Some relationships do need to end, but most can be moved out a sphere or two to create a healthy distance.

Sharing feelings is the most intimate exchange we have with people. Reducing intimacy with someone involves decreasing the amount of feeling communication you have with him or her. Sharing your thoughts and opinions can be reduced, as can the amount of time you spend together. There are those who will challenge you on the new boundaries you set. Being challenged is fine—most of us need time to adjust to changes initiated by others. Violations are not fine. Whether emotional, mental, or physical, those of us committed to growing our inner light each day cannot have any abuse in our lives.

Stating, "I'm uncomfortable with being spoken to that way. I need to go now," provides both words and actions. People take time to learn. End every conversation that becomes disrespectful if it can't redirect itself immediately. Others will soon understand that in order to have a relationship with you they need to be respectful.

Some Bright Ones have difficulty distancing themselves from loved ones. This is understandable, because being filled with energy equates to being filled with love. However, the truth is that honoring ourselves *is* honoring others at the energy or spirit level. When someone violates you they are attempting to steal your energy. By not giving it to them you teach them to connect to their own energy.

Although it might be challenging for you, as a bright light, to gain distance or move closer to certain people, the initial tension you feel will quickly be replaced with expansiveness and joy. By carefully choosing who you do and do not allow into your inner circle of intimacy, you learn to trust the person who is ultimately responsible for keeping you safe and loved: you. Honoring yourself allows you to become a lighthouse for those striving to do the same.

Forgiveness

Forgiveness is the process of bringing energy back into your body. For those of us who have not achieved sainthood, this process is organic and takes time. There is a lot of talk about "letting go," encouraging us to move on from our grievances as soon as possible. It is liberating when you get to the point of reclaiming that last bit of your energy after being hurt, but, placing too much emphasis on moving on and letting go puts us in danger of glossing over a process that, although painful, ultimately makes us new again.

Because we are housed in physical bodies and become emotionally attached to other physical bodies, whenever we get hurt, the energetic attachment is damaged. In some instances, the task is to repair the connection to another. In other instances, the task is to reclaim the energy and integrate it back into your body, thereby releasing all emotional attachment to the other person.

Enlightened ones—those who are bright beyond belief—are full of light because they are detached. They love completely, yet without sending energetic strings to tie onto the other person. Their energy remains with them. They certainly give and receive energy, yet it is without attachment or expectation.

The stronger the attachment to another person, the longer it will take to integrate the energy back into your body. This is an organic process that, again, takes time. We can assist the process by being aware of and experiencing our feelings, and by talking to those who are supportive. Conversely, we can hinder the process by denying that forgiveness needs to occur. Denial requires distraction from self, and we are certainly capable of doing this for a time, but not forever.

Any time you have a lingering grievance that you choose to ignore rather than feel and forgive, you lose energy. If you have 10 lingering grievances, you lose energy through each of them.

Energy Tip: Get a piece of paper and write down every insult or hurt you can remember. Vow to feel the feelings and release the offense as soon as possible. You know you have forgiven when the mental memory of the incident no longer elicits an emotional response.

Sometimes we unconsciously choose not to process and forgive a situation because we fear the result. The following is a list of some common reasons people don't forgive.

- ﹏ A belief that forgiving gives permission for the person to do it again.
- ﹏ A belief that forgiveness condones the act.
- ﹏ An unconscious fear that processing the feelings will end the relationship.
- ﹏ An investment in being a victim (attention from others, and so on).

True forgiveness entails accepting feelings that are painful. It's no wonder that so many of us don't want to go through the anguish of feeling betrayed, judged, disrespected, and so forth. Emotional safety is required to heal. Therefore, if the person who hurt you is still around and is not helping you heal, you are in an environment that is hostile to your emotional self. Emotional or physical distance is often necessary if you do not have support and empathy from the person who hurt you.

Very often society promotes the idea that forgiveness should be granted without hesitation. If we are to rebuild a healthy connection, support from the other person to help you forgive is in order. If the person is judgmental of you, or unwilling to "talk about the past," it may be time to get some distance so that you can honor yourself and heal.

The safer your relationships the more you can love unconditionally while remaining grounded and connected to your internal source of energy. We are responsible for creating emotional and physical safety for ourselves. If those around us are loving and supportive that is wonderful—if not, you'll want to ask yourself if you prefer the security and familiarity of a nonsupportive, situation to the unknown experience of transformation that leads to brightness and empowerment.

Nourishing Relationships

When you first meet someone and fall in love, whether it's the love of your life or your newborn baby, energy surges through you—and them—resulting in an explosion of love so intense you could burst.

The relationship develops as an entity—unseen though easily sensed. It feels safe and warm. It is ultimate comfort. Love overflows from your union, buffering the blows of everyday life during the first few years of a relationship. Through time, we get used to the comforts of our relationships and come to them often for balm and bliss.

Once the initial ecstasy of a new relationship wears off, so does the velocity of love energy pouring through your system. The love doesn't go away—it simply changes from a rapid river to a flowing stream. At this point, because the process is so gradual, it is common to be unaware that the delicate balance of your relationship has shifted. In the midst of innocent oblivion, one continues to go to the relationship to supplement his own energy reserves. Time passes and, if we're not aware of this process, more energy flows out of the relationship than into it, causing an imbalance.

This is when you find yourself in a power struggle. It may appear as verbal banter about who is busier or more exhausted, or who is doing more than the other around the house. In truth, it is an indication that your relationship is low on energy and needs replenishing. But, more importantly, the individuals in the relationship need replenishing—from within. It has become a habit to get energy from the relationship, but at some point we need to dig our roots deep into our own wells and reconnect to our own sources. Only then can we bring fresh energy to our union.

When we don't know the real cause of the problem, we say that we are having "communication issues," or perhaps, "money issues." Deep down it is almost always a power and energy issue.

We connect with one another physically, mentally, emotionally, and spiritually. It is important to have the ability to exchange energy and come together on each of these levels. However, all the intellectual conversation in the world will not bring new energy into your relationships; it will simply recycle what's already there. You may have had the experience of going to each other to "talk," and feeling as if you are trying to suck life out of what has become a stone. Verbal exchange is fantastic and fun and does not need to be avoided; however, it is *being* rather than *doing* that infuses life into your relationship. If you can talk mindfully, with compassion and deep listening, you are nourishing the relationship while talking.

Nourishing a relationship is as important as nourishing oneself, but if we are depleted, we have nothing to give. Relationships are in flux right now because we have lifestyles of chronic depletion. Writing lists about what needs to be done and sharing a quick meal together does not provide the space needed to fill your relationship with energy. Just as mindful awareness, rather than obsessive thinking, infuses your body with energy, being with one another in stillness fills the well with a potentially infinite amount of energy, compassion, creativity, and joy—or, in a word, love.

Energy Tip: Dedicate 15 minutes a day to *being* with your loved one. Before you speak or share feelings, spend a few moments sitting hand in hand, or wrapped in each other's arms. Connect with your breath and his or her breath—you will sense your relationship being charged with life.

Making room for spiritual connection in your relationship is the key to regeneration. Have you ever noticed someone really looking at you? You look up and notice eyes upon you and know that they are seeing you—really seeing you—for who you are at the deepest level. For the one looking, it is as if a veil is lifted and he or she gets a glimpse of a glorious human being. For the one being seen, it is like receiving the most fantastic gift you can imagine. This brings presence, spirit, energy, or being into your relationship. Just as meditation in the morning creates a buffer against minor irritations that arise throughout the day, bringing spiritual presence into your relationship lifts it to a level of effortless ease and joy.

Endings

Most of us are still getting used to applying laws of life—energy—to major life decisions. Decisions are made differently when energy flow is used to measure success in work, relationships, or any given aspect of your life. Because we get attached to constants in our environment, cultivating the ability to release these constants when necessary is crucial to staying energized.

Whenever motivation is brought down to the lowest common denominator, we find love and fear. Fear would have us hold on tight—until vested in the work retirement account, or perhaps, until "death do us part." Love—what we feel when energy is flowing—would have us follow it around like an improvised dance.

The other day a woman in her early 50s asked me why her intuition seemed to be fading. I told her that whenever one can't hear one's own voice it's because there is a message one is trying to ignore. You can't ignore one piece of intuition and clearly tune in to the rest. Unfortunately, it just doesn't work that way. The energy flowing through us sometimes brings information that is difficult to reconcile with conventional wisdom. It might urge you to get some space from your husband or wife in order to reconnect with yourself, or to take action regarding another situation in life that you would rather avoid.

Being a clear and open vessel for life energy brings joy and fulfillment beyond any expectation because we are designed for the purpose of immense self-expression. However, it sometimes brings endings as well. The voice of life asks us to be willing to leave a situation or relationship if it is not supporting our growth or ever-increasing self-expression. Here is the good news: sometimes being willing to leave is all that is required. In these cases, the willingness opens you up internally so that life can move through and dissolve your fear of leaving. Once the fear is dissolved, your lesson is over and your intuition guides you to stay in the relationship, if you'd like.

Other times, once you have moved through the fear, you will still feel an urge to move on. Sitting on this urge, or staying in a situation that no longer supports your growth, leads to your energy turning against itself. This is where self-destructive behavior comes into the picture. You can only ignore the urgings of life for so long without having to go numb. Excessive eating, drinking, shopping, working, or any form of distraction will do.

Energy Tip: Check for sabotaging behaviors. Ask yourself what the behavior is distracting you from, and be prepared to listen. Thank it for serving you well before releasing it from duty.

Insight into your behavior is step one, *action toward honoring yourself* is step two. If you do not take action, the sabotaging behavior will return to you once again.

Endings are for warriors. It takes courage and conviction to end a part of your life to which you are attached. It also takes having an identity grounded in the current of life. I know it sounds like an oxymoron—grounding in the current—but it is truly the only form of security that exists. Holding on to a branch by the stream because you're afraid of the rapids is merely procrastination.

Tuning in to your one point of reference to see if you should end a relationship, or any part of your life, is essential, but can be challenging. The voice of life is often drowned out with overbearing voices telling us that commitment is forever, that to leave is failure... If leaving is the right thing, and you are sincerely open to doing the right thing, you will one day have the inner conviction you need. Your inner voice will be heard loud and clear. Ending a relationship is hard even when it's the right thing to do. You will refer to that inner conviction over and over again as your rational mind and social self questions your decision. Bottom line: wait for conviction before making any decision of this magnitude.

All endings, regardless of whether it is of a partnership, job, or friendship, should occur in the spirit of kindness and compassion. When such endings are urged by life, a mindful ending is natural. Endings are harsh only when the ego gets involved. When you feel an ending is in order, allow the process to be organic rather than reactive. This way everyone involved will emerge sad but not damaged.

Your partner or others who are involved may become mean-spirited or unkind. All we can do is try our best to remain mindful rather than become reactive. Keeping your end "clean" means that you are not spewing contaminated energy onto others. It also means that you have less to clean up later. Whatever they spew will be their responsibility. Grieving fully within your self is the best way to deal with the messy emotions that often come up with endings. Sometimes the kindest thing we can do for ourselves is sit at home and cry, listen to some music, or watch a movie that honors whatever you are feeling at the time. Music and movies are great for helping emotional energy move through your system.

Work

The world of work is undergoing a radical transformation. Some of us are choosing to work for ourselves; others are choosing to bring their light into organizations each day. Organizations are in desperate need of Bright Ones. Transforming from old-world business structures to a more modern empowerment model is an arduous process for these complex systems. Whenever an individual, system, or institution heads toward transformation, it engenders much fear. This is unavoidable and expected, because, by definition, transformation involves partial death before new life is able to emerge.

Charged employees in the workplace feel, more than their duller counterparts, the tension of dissonance that exists in most organizations today. We are challenged to find ways to bring our energies and spirits into the workplace, for leaving them at home is far too costly—the price is a divided life, which is energetically devastating. There is no way to be fully energized at home and on the weekends, but not at work. There is no way to work all year toward a vacation designed to keep you going for the rest of the year. Being bright and filled with life energy is a daily commitment that must be applied across the board to every aspect of life. Of course, there are those activities that are less fun than others, but having severe energy shifts that rise and fall depending on what you are doing, is like being on an energetic roller coaster which is inherently draining.

With that said, what are Bright Ones doing to maintain their energy in today's changing workplace? In four words, the answer is *purpose, management, expression,* and *choice.*

Those of you who are energized in the workplace are able to connect your work for to a higher purpose. The purpose might range from helping those around you, to learning valuable skills so that you are able to move forward. Ideally, you will be in a job that you feel is matched with your natural talents and therefore supports authentic self-expression. It also helps to respect the values of the organization of which you are a member. Current research on organizational culture shows that your immediate peers and work groups are more tied to job satisfaction than the quality of executive-level leadership. If you work for the most positive organization on the planet, but have a toxic supervisor, you will be more adversely affected than if you have a wonderful supervisor in a struggling organization. Certainly feeling supported by the people in your immediate work group goes a long way toward being fulfilled at work.

The next is management—energy management of course. Managing your energy so that it does not get drained by workplace gossip or bureaucratic proce-dures involves having impeccable integrity at work. You may notice that your bright coworkers do not bad-mouth others or participate in negative communication channels. A good rule of thumb is not to say *anything* to anyone at work that you wouldn't feel comfortable with others knowing. The reason for this limited level of openness (or appropriate boundaries, really) is that wondering if other people know what you said, or if they are going to tell someone what you said, takes tons of energy—the price you pay is becoming dull and dissatisfied.

Multitasking brings to mind efficiency, but when it comes to managing your energy, multitasking is not al-ways the best choice. Doing many things at once tends to fragment one's energy—we lose the quality of present moment focus. A synergistic effect occurs when we engage our minds, hearts, and bodies all at the same time. This level of attention lends itself to finding creative solu-tions in the moment with little or no mistakes in record-breaking speed—how's that for efficiency?

A daily spiritual practice is also an essential energy management strategy. It doesn't take long to connect with your core before leaving for work. Sit yourself down and visualize your body charging like a cell phone. You'll know when you're good to go!

Energy Tip: The next time a tense situation at work arises, pull your energy into your body and connect to your core by taking several full breaths. This will buffer you from losing large amounts of energy in one daily crisis.

Ultimately the transformation of an organization has to be a grassroots movement. Your part involves using your voice and expressing yourself when you have something to say. A major reason that people are unsatisfied at work is because they are sitting on their own energy by keeping their mouths shut. This does not serve the individual or the organization. Of course, diplomacy is critical. One can't just complain or vent in an unproductive way. If you're not convinced that you have the skills to express yourself in a way that is productive, enroll in an interpersonal communications class at your local college. Think of your connection with the organization for which you work as a relationship—energetically, it is. If we continuously hold on to our thoughts and feelings, eventually we will blow or go. Those are the only two outcomes of chronic lack of self-expression. Express yourself!

Finally, knowing that you have a choice is crucial for staying energized at work. If you find yourself in a chronically toxic environment, committing to yourself that you can leave the job, regardless of the size of your paycheck, is essential. This empowering mindset actually results in a higher level of commitment and job satisfaction than feeling like a victim of your circumstances. Knowing that it is your choice to be there despite the imperfection of it all gives you power from within.

We spend such a large amount of time working. Being able to contribute to something larger than ourselves is very fulfilling. As you contribute, you express, and as you know, this is how you fill yourself with energy from the inside out.

Sustainable Living

Looking at life from an energetic perspective necessitates a view that includes both nourishment and sustainability. Being mindful of the laws of energy requires that we approach life in a way that supports renewal.

It is possible—for a time—to blindly suck the life out of everything: ourselves, each other, and Mother Earth. Sadly, we have been taking more than giving for a long time. The price we pay individually is anxiety, depression, illness, and addiction. Relationally, we struggle and ultimately go our separate ways, and environmentally, the earth trembles with despair. Illness, divorce, and natural disaster, begging us to pay attention to how we live our lives.

We are waking up. One by one, we make decisions that support sustainability. If depletion is the cause of all of the previously mentioned symptoms, nourishment is the cure. As we nourish ourselves, we approach life full rather than empty. Our choices center on what feeds us instead of what drains us. At the level of spirit, what feeds you also feeds your neighbors and the world. Therefore, the first step toward creating a sustainable world is to make sure that you are not operating on an energy deficit. This fullness overflows into your relationships as well.

At the level of spirit and energy, everything is one. Still, today, a collective "us and them" paradigm exists. We spend a tremendous amount of time and energy blaming other people, countries, and ethnicities for the world's problems, often forgetting that we all share the same delicate planet. Those of us attuned to energy are seeing that nothing separates us from one another or from the earth and heavens. We have mistreated the earth in a self-serving manner, and one by one we are waking up to the fact that it cannot occur a moment longer.

Many of us are modifying the way we live to be more in harmony with nature. The more people who are mindful of creating a sustainable environment, the more quickly the behavior will catch on. Look around you—what are you doing to support renewal? Here are some ideas:

- ❧ Purchase from organizations that are concerned about the environment.

- ❧ Clean your home with environmentally friendly products to reduce your own toxic waste.

- ❧ Buy less.

- ❧ Live close to work, take public transportation, or drive a hybrid automobile.

- ❧ Recycle and give away household items often.

- ❧ Donate to charities that assist those less fortunate to develop ways to care for themselves—for example, building wells instead of giving water.

- ❧ Buy organic food.

- ❧ Support leaders and groups who practice and support sustainability.

This list could be a book in itself. There are so many things that each of us could do to contribute to sustainability of the planet. Each conscious choice that you make feeds energy into the collective consciousness. It will reach a tipping point, and the masses will embrace sustainable living.

When we choose to see ourselves as separate from each other, we remain blind to a piece of ourselves. It is a form of denial that dampens your energy system. Your brightness cannot occur in a vacuum. Extending compassion to all of life through conscious choices opens your vessel to receive, contain, and express ever more energy.

Energy Tip: Create more, buy less. The energy you seek lives within you.

We live in a consumption-driven society. Those able to stop over-consuming are spiritual leaders who are intuitive and connected. I am not suggesting that we walk around wearing potato sacks—I enjoy beautiful shoes as much as the next girl. However, buying to fill a hole is destructive to oneself and the environment. The truth is that if we are all mindful, there is enough to go around.

Simply ask yourself, "Do I really want this?" If the answer is yes, go for it, and perhaps give away something that you already have to keep the energy flowing. If you feel a little tension in your tummy, you may want to wait and see if you still want the item in a day or two.

Remember to keep your surroundings simple, and not to collect too much stuff. Minimal is good—excess clutter is an indication that you're internally weighed down. Sometimes getting rid of the stuff is a catalyst for releasing internal energy blocks that you may be holding onto for selfprotection, or for a (false) sense of security.

Be free within and celebrate that all life is connected. Try blessing the trees around your home for the beauty they provide—you may be surprised when you hear them say "Thank you!"

Everyday Choices

Each day you are presented with hundreds of choices about how to spend your time, your money—about how to distribute your energy wisely. Time and money are energy currencies and should be valued as such. If you waste either, you pour energy from your system. If you are stingy with either, you hold tightly to your energy, constricting the flow.

Here is a secret energy principle: Value your time and money and you will have a lot of each. Monitor your energy each time you are presented with a choice about how to schedule your time or spend your money. It will unequivocally tell you. If you listen, it will guide you toward financial abundance and days with enough time to do all that is truly important to you.

Energy communicates with us in many ways. First, if you are doing anything out of "obligation," rather than inspiration, you are not in alignment with the flow of life. Quickly find a way to modify that activity or expense.

If when you leave someone you feel drained, depleted, confused, or agitated, ask yourself why. The relationship may be in need of a change. On the other hand, if you find yourself feeling light-hearted and free when leaving someone or someplace, you have spent your time and energy wisely.

At some level you know that choices made by consulting your energy or intuition benefit everyone. Keep in mind the levels of self: spiritual, emotional, mental, and physical. It is not uncommon for people to emotionally, mentally, or physically react to your intuitive choices. This does not mean that you are being selfish or making the wrong decisions; it means that they are resisting their own growth and that you need to stand firm in your guidance.

No one ever maintained brightness by doing things to please others at the expense of himself. I recently saw an interview with a successful film producer. When asked how he makes decisions on what movie to work on, he said, "I always choose movies that I would go to myself. I would never make a movie based on what the public wants." He is wise. By choosing to follow his heart and own interests, he is making brilliant movies that speak strongly to certain people, rather than weakly to the masses. When too much focus is placed on what others want, our energy becomes diluted and the effect is no longer profound.

Energy management is intuitive living. It is an inside-out approach to life—addressing the cause and not the symptoms. When we make decisions from the outside in, based on what we think we should do or what others want us to do, we simply move around energy that is already out there. It takes courage to live at the level of source, bringing fresh, creative energy into the world, but it is so worthwhile. Every decision you make that honors your thoughts and feelings will increase your brightness.

Energy Tip: Take an inventory of your choices during the course of one day. Acknowledge yourself for making choices that energize you. Look carefully at those that don't, and ask yourself how to change the situation. Once you get an answer—it may take a day or two—follow through with making a change.

You may be aware that something you're doing is not honoring your deepest self, and at the same time fear the consequences of making a change. There is no doubt that certain situations or relationships sometimes fall apart when they are not being supported in the way that they are used to. Inside-out living takes courage. Talk to yourself daily about the truth. Life will support you through any transformation that arises from honoring life. You are the light of the world.

Chapter 6

Increase Your Passion!

Passion, enthusiastic interest in someone or something, brings your journey toward luminosity full circle. The first five sections (connecting to your core, and the energy of feelings, thoughts, physical body, and environment) help you receive and contain energy in a self-supporting way. Passion directs your energy and keeps it moving toward the object of your affection. It doesn't matter what the object is—how significant or seemingly frivolous, What matters is that you are keenly interested.

You, who are fully charged, find yourself passionate about many things: people, life's work, hobbies, music, nature, and more. Being passionate is a key component of being bright. Even those who don't take the time to connect to their core each day feel alive when their energy is directed toward meaningful activities.

For those of you who feed your passions every day—congratulations. Adding the other energy management techniques to your already stoked fire will take you to even higher levels of brightness.

For those of you who are reading this and wondering how you can feed your passion when you don't even have enough energy to exercise, be compassionate with yourself. As you bring more energy into your system by applying the tips in the first chapters of the book, your body will naturally respond by perking up around people or interests that may ultimately be recipients of your passion.

Notice subtle shifts in your energy when you hear your favorite song, or perhaps (as recently occurred with a client) while reading an article on solar energy, for your dancing cells will lead you toward your passions.

Look to ignite your passions in the following sections:

- Follow Your Heart
- Becoming Edgy
- Your Archetypal Blueprint
- Funky Spirituality
- Sex
- Laughter
- Pleasure

Follow Your Heart

Love is the language of the heart, and a major energy source. We can all identify with being "passionately in love", your heart is wide open and love pours through to your beloved. The idea is to fall passionately in love with life—this is both the outcome and the process of energy management. For being in love leads to maximum expression, and maximum expression feels like being in love.

A children's book called *Me First and the Gimme Gimmes* by Gerald Jampolsky and Diane Cirincione (Health Communications, 1991), brilliantly illustrates the journey toward heart-based expression. Before the "Gimme Gimme folk" learn to follow their hearts, they have huge heads and spend all their time and energy competing for outside resources. They are lonely and desperate.

In some ways, the book parallels the story about how *A Course in Miracles* came about. The *Course* is a book on spiritual psychotherapy. It includes self-guided lessons that teach us to look at life through the eyes of love. Seeds for the *Course* were planted when a contentious group of psychology professors became tired of the "angry and aggressive" feelings between them. One day the head of the department said in exasperation, "There must be another way." Two members of the faculty joined together to find that other way. The collaboration between them set the stage for Helen Schucman to begin receiving the messages that would eventually, with the help of William Thetford, become *A Course in Miracles*, a comprehensive and accelerated spiritual guide to following your heart.

In the children's book, one of the Gimme Gimmes climbs to the top of the mountain one day out of sheer desperation and declares, "There must be another way." He then he hears a loving voice from deep inside that turns out to be the voice of his heart. It urges him to use his heart as a guide for a new way to live based on love and joy rather than competition and blame. His heart says, "I'll be your guide, so *listen* to me—I'll show you the road to a new way to be."

Our hearts ache with the desire to lead us to a life of fulfillment, pleasure, and joy. There is only one catch: If we are holding on to grievances, our hearts will be heavy and unable to speak loud enough for us to hear. We need not let people who have hurt us back into our lives in order to release a grievance. Just be willing to look at the pain you are holding on to. Looking at it will lead to feeling it—and feeling it leads to releasing it. Again, your body will only be able to fully release old pain if you have removed yourself from toxic and damaging situations. If you are still in them, your body will need to remain defended.

Energy Tip: Make a date with your heart…just the two of you. Out loud, tell it that you are ready to listen to whatever it has to say. Be willing to shed a few tears; there is not a heart among us that's not heavy with unreleased sadness. Once your heart lightens, it will buoyantly lead you to your passionate destiny.

Many of us guard our hearts with slumped shoulders or unconscious shields, which offer a form of pseudo-protection. The protection seeks to keep you from your own pain. Letting old pain wash over you is crucial to increasing your energy capacity. Once our hearts are healed, energy pours through, carrying the vibration of love. There is no higher vibration—it fills us with essential nourishment, and blesses the world many times over.

To accelerate this process, focus on bringing love into every situation and interaction. Also, deliberately bring pleasure into your life. Wear clothes that you love, eat what you love, do what you love, spend time with people you love, love the beauty around you.

Put your hand on your heart and feel it get warm and tingly with energy. Your heart is a powerful energy force, and it will expand very quickly with your permission. Be prepared to be bathed in love as the energy moves in and through your heart center.

As your heart opens up, you will be guided toward your passions one step at a time. Your inner guidance may or may not make sense at first. You may feel a longing to become a musician at the age of 50. You might be inspired to volunteer at a local charity, despite feeling exhausted. As the authors of *Me First and the Gimme Gimmes* so eloquently say, "RIGHT FROM THE START FOLLOW YOUR HEART!"

Becoming Edgy

You know when you contain a lot of energy because your presence sharpens with intensity and you develop a palpable edge or border. Each time you honor the one point of reference within you, you infuse your being with energy. As you make choices that reflect your true feelings, energy rushes from your core into each of your cells and into the energy field that surrounds your body.

The upside of claiming and honoring your authentic self is empowerment and brightness. The downside is that sometimes being true to your core conflicts with other people's agendas. That is when you feel your edge. And they feel your edge. You bump up against each other's edges and choose not to cave in on yourself.

It takes time to get used to this feeling—you may already be proficient, or you may still be affected by others' will to shape and define you, but choose not to give in to their expectations. Or, you may be empowered as long as it doesn't offend, but when it does, you give your power away in order to "keep peace." Wherever you are in this process of becoming edgy, know that it's a good thing—powerful and transformative.

Because a mass of energy equals power, we need to be comfortable with the feeling of being powerful. Women in particular are socialized to connect with others, to cultivate rapport and seek consensus; this is great, though sometimes done to extreme. Feeling the need to connect with everyone can lead to abandoning oneself. The good news is that we can join with others on the level of spirit or energy without agreeing with their opinions or liking their personalities. Joining at this level is simply acknowledging the very real truth that we are one.

Connecting at the level of spirit or energy, but not at an emotional or intellectual level, involves remaining open and nonjudgmental. Your essence remains expansive from your core or solar plexus area, but is contained at an emotional or intellectual level. Managing your energy in such a way allows you to remain connected to your core and to maintain your personal power in the face of seeming adversity.

Energy Tip: The next time you disagree with someone's words or actions, attempt to stay spiritually connected with them while speaking your truth. Notice how you feel as you validate their essence in the midst of a disagreement.

Being powerful from the inside out is very different from depending upon externally derived power, to which some people become addicted. External power in the form of money and status can be intoxicating. Those who are unaware of the ultimately disempowering effects of external power sometimes identify with it as their source and attempt to get it at their own or another's expense.

You may find that, as your internal power increases, people want to give you more time, attention, and energy. However, an internally powerful person knows that to rely on the energy coming from others, or to use it as the drug that it can be, will temporarily disconnect us from our sources. Engaging in an external "energy binge" always requires us to reconnect with our core later, causing a lull while the flow reverses from outside-in to inside-out.

The people who are used to you being at a certain voltage may react negatively as your internal power increases. In fact, this experience is fairly universal and can be terrifying. Some will adjust to you, and others will not. It may be helpful to view it as a social reorganization. Those who are not able to adjust to you becoming more authentically you, and therefore more powerful and less malleable, will try to undermine your growth with their fears. Most often, those who are uncomfortable with our brightness are sitting on their own energy. The best thing we can do for them, ourselves, and everyone else, is to keep beaming. As you continue to get brighter and brighter every day, the tension that your brightness causes in others may ultimately lead them to connect to their own internal energy source.

Each of us has a part to play in the collective transformation of society. Your role is to be you. That's it! To nourish your spirit, honor yourself, and express your passions—to align with the authentically shaped container that you were given to express universal energy.

The path of passion increases your energy rapidly. As you brighten, others feel your energy, presence, or edge more strongly. You will find that you are a bigger wave in the ocean, so to speak. Worry not; as your energy expands, you will gently learn how to approach others with compassion without diminishing your authentic power. Be prepared though. It is rare to traverse this passionate path without ruffling a couple of feathers along the way. Consider it a sign that you are moving in the right direction.

Your Archetypal Blueprint

Embracing and cultivating your personal style generates passion. Each of us is born with an archetypal blueprint awaiting our acceptance. Before wondering if you are in the right career or living your purpose, identify your archetypal blueprint.

You can do this by identifying the major aspects of your personality since birth. You are like a diamond. Each facet is one aspect of your archetype. Each facet has sub-facets. For example, the four major facets of my archetypal blueprint are Healer, Lover, Teacher, and Visionary. Each of these has a more specific list below it like writer, mother, and so on.

Upon learning about archetypal blueprints, my sister-in-law Amy asked me to help her identify the facets of her personality. Intuitively, we came up with the following four facets: Hippie, Artist, Planner, and Friend.

Amy shared that simply acknowledging herself at this level felt empowering. She also realized that she always felt that she wanted to be artistic, though didn't think she had what it takes. Amy realized that she had limited the definition to visual art, which isn't her gift. However, for the past four years, Amy has put together a Christmas CD for all her friends and family, which is a compilation of all her favorite songs for the year. Once she acknowledged the part of herself that is an artist, she was able to see all the creative things she already does in her life.

As we identify, claim, and integrate each facet, we become shiny and radiant like a diamond. Identifying your archetypal blueprint is an intuitive process. You can start by centering yourself with a few mindful breaths. You may want to light a candle and state the intention to identify your archetypal blueprint. Have a journal handy. Close your eyes and see what major categories come to you. Do not—I repeat—do not dismiss anything that comes to you. When Amy heard the word *hippie*, she initially said, "That couldn't be the name of an archetype…" But it kept coming up for her until she claimed it. There are no right or wrong archetype facets. They range from *rebel* to *mother* to *mediator* to *designer*. Let your intuition guide you. You may also want to brainstorm various aspects of your authentic self in your journal. Write word after word, and when you're done, see what words feel like category headings (facets), and which feel like subheadings (sub-facets).

Your archetypal blueprint has nothing to do with your "issues." It has more to do with the aspects of your personality that you brought into this world. As you identify, claim, and integrate each facet of your archetypal blueprint, you naturally express these gifts more and more every day, thereby becoming increasingly refined and radiant.

This is where your personal style comes into the picture. The goal is to "embody your archetype," as my intuition so clearly stated upon contemplation of this topic. Most of us do this somewhat without even knowing it. The idea is to be bold and proud about expressing and demonstrating your essence.

Think of the people you admire most—famous or not—and notice how fully they embody their essence. Is it reflected in their work, hobbies, and personal style?

Now, get to work figuring out your own. If there is a type of person that you consistently find yourself admiring, it may be that they embody an archetypal facet that you have not yet claimed.

Cultivating your personal style to accurately reflect your archetypal blueprint is an important way of expressing your essence. Our modern popular culture tends to condition us to be clones. I can't think of anything more disempowering than adopting a style that is externally prescribed.

Energy Tip: Evaluate your things, including your wardrobe, car, and items in your home. The things that most reflect you will make you smile. Donate the items that don't reflect who you are— they will reflect someone else's essence!

Once we embrace our essence there is nothing left to do but express it—in doing so, we become powerful from the inside out, inspiring others to move toward their own brilliance. No two of us are alike—the world needs each of us to be bold, sparkly, and powerful in our own way.

Funky Spirituality

There's nothing like a funky song to get me in touch with my spiritual nature. Not the kind of spirituality that's detached from the senses, but rather, a sensual, even sexy version. For me, reggae or hip-hop does the trick—for you it may be rock and roll or classical. Whatever your preference, music magically connects your spiritual essence to your body and to the world simultaneously.

Modern spirituality is upon us. Being charged in this world requires that we be fully in it, which is paradoxical to traditional spiritual wisdom. A tapestry of raw spirit and refined skill weave themselves together to create embodied spirituality.

Every art form, including music, is infused with the emotion of the artist at the time it was created. If a musician is a clear vessel through which perfect melodies are channeled, that is brilliant and will illicit a similar feeling in listeners. However, even when a musician is angry and hurt, the core energy permeating the sometimes violent lyrics can be healing. It's healing to the musician and to the listeners with similar emotional landscapes. It is fascinating to watch an angry musician throughout the course his or her career. At come point you can feel that the raw anger has been processed and the work begins to take on a new tone. Core expression of spiritual energy does that.

The magic of music comes from the alchemic effect of pure spiritual energy moving through the musician's emotional landscape and through a sharply defined container or polished skill set. When you hear it, intensity arises as you resonate with the artist's essence and feelings imbedded in the music.

As we know, feeling intense emotions is required in order to release them. Music can help us do this. You may notice that sometimes you are in the mood for a certain type of music, and other times you want something different. Honor your intuition in this—it knows what vibration your body needs, to perhaps process a certain emotion, or to connect with a certain aspect of yourself.

Energy Tip: Put a dozen of your favorite CDs in front of you. Ask yourself which songs you're in the mood for. Notice the feelings that stir within you as you listen. Do you feel inspired, sad, or angry? No need to analyze the origin of the feelings— simply let the music move you.

Each of us is an artist in our own way, in that we all creatively express energy toward objects of passion. Think of anything at which you are particularly skilled, and you will discover your unique artistic brand. You may be brilliant at cooking or arranging things to look beautiful. Or perhaps you have a more left-brained skill such as working with numbers. Artistic expression is always a combination of left- and right-brain functioning. If your particular gift is more linear or left-brain, the right side of your brain kicks in to help you express it in your own way. If your brand of artistic expression is right-brained by nature, your left brain is required to help you organize the expression.

Integration is the key here—the integration of spirit and matter, left brain and right brain, body and soul, intuition and reason. The idea is to bring this level of refined expression into every aspect of life. No longer do we need to wait for a vacation or a good concert to get energized. We ourselves become integrated, and each moment becomes an artistic expression of life.

Music is a beautiful illustration of integration. Because of this, it integrates us as we listen to it. We are so blessed to live in a culture that celebrates music the way that it does. Now go get your groove on.

Sex

Is there anything more associated with passion than sex? Sex is the ultimate act of creation, and the foundation of passion. Sexual energy is primal and bubbles up from the ground of our being. This procreative essence is a primary source of fuel, whether channeled during lovemaking or directed upward toward expression in other areas of life.

You do not have to be having sex to benefit from the energy that flows from your sexual center. In fact, many mystical teachings recommend abstinence as a way to become more energized. Then again, so is fasting...

Sex, making love, passionate union, or whatever you want to call it, is glorious, and imbues one's body with dancing atoms of light. You can almost see the sparkling specks surrounding newly in-love couples.

Conversely, I've noticed in my practice that clients who have lost their lust for life experience a diminished sex drive. This makes sense because it is all related—passion is passion. It is impossible to sit on your passion (deny that which brings you joy) for an extended period of time and not have it dampen the flame of your sexual desire. Simply spending some time doing what you love will ignite the flame once again.

There are some guidelines for passion-generating sex. Choosing not to follow these guidelines does not make one "bad," but simply leaves energetic consequences. The mantra for passion-generating sex is this: If it's not right, it's not worth it.

So what is right? Consider this: Your energy centers open and expand when you engage in sexual activity. This expansiveness, combined with the physical nature of sex, pumps energy into your system. Given this information, there are two things to consider. First, when your energy system and body are open, you literally exchange energy with the other person. Therefore, ask yourself if his essence will bring you down or elevate you. If she is emotionally or physically toxic, you are taking on that toxicity and vise versa. If they are bright, healthy, and loving, you receive an incredible gift.

Next, you'll want to ask yourself how you feel about each other. If it is a loveless relationship, you can "have sex" for the sake of sex only, though you'll likely open only your sexual centers and not connect at the heart or other levels. This may or may not be fine for you. You'll want to intuitively ask your body, mind, spirit, and emotional self if you're paying an energy price or not.

Many people have shared stories of crying during or after sex. If you are in an unhealthy relationship, feelings of sadness may release as you open up and increase the velocity of energy moving through your body. Tears bring information—ask them what they would like you to know—is it, perhaps, time to go?

Sexual addiction is on the rise, as are all addictions, due to the consumption-oriented society we've created. You may have some addictive tendencies concerning sex. If, for example, you find yourself becoming agitated when you don't get your way, or tend to compromise your integrity to get your needs met, then you have an untamed animal on your hands. This is an opportunity for refinement.

Like every other addiction, sexual addiction is primal energy that has been fed, on demand, one too many times, and consequently has a life of its own. Think of it as a spoiled child and offer it the discipline it needs. Simply sit on the energy next time it arises—pardon the pun. Allow yourself to be frustrated. In time it will turn into more refined energy, and the addictive part of your desire will dissipate. After a few times of doing this, you will be in charge of it instead of the other way around.

Healthy sexuality is ultimately fulfilling. If you find yourself in a relationship with someone you love and value who feels the same about you, celebrate, for you are blessed.

Energy Tip: Read this chapter with your beloved. Prior to making love, vow to open all of your energy centers, from the base of your spine to the top of your head. Go slowly and experience the pleasure of a whole-body orgasm.

We are, by nature, sexual beings, but many families carry shame around sexuality. If you come from a family that considers sex "dirty," or if, on the other hand, you had the serious misfortune of having someone in your family who was sexually inappropriate or abusive, feel the feelings around that.

Most people have at least some repressed sexual energy. Integrating this energy is the goal, as it makes you whole and strong and vital. Simply intending to integrate any energy repressed due to shame or abuse will cause it to surface. You may find yourself having wild dreams. Dreams are good—they help us look at, and feel, what we need in order to become more integrated.

As we claim our sexual natures and accept and love our bodies more, our journeys to brightness will be fueled with this powerful, yet refined, primal energy.

Laughter

When was the last time you laughed hysterically—holding your stomach, snorting (if you're the snorting kind...), and letting out a big sigh at the end to regain your equilibrium? Laughter is the energy of joy bubbling to the surface as it tickles your cells. What a wonderful feeling to have a good laugh.

Patch Adams was on to something when he used humor to heal. Joy is one face of spiritual energy, and spiritual energy is fundamentally healing. When we laugh we bring loads of energy into our systems. For this reason, and for the sheer fun of it, laughter is worth cultivating.

This past year my sister made a New Year's resolution to laugh more—what a wonderful way to start a year! In fact, our intention is often all that is required to invoke a particular quality of energy such as laughter. You see, it is already there within us and can be tapped into at any moment.

I've noticed something rather profound about laughter and the expression of positive emotions in general. The clearer your physical system—the less congested with toxins—the easier it is for these higher energy vibrations to bubble up. It seems that when we are bogged down physically, emotional energy also gets a bit heavy. Lower energy frequencies yield feelings such as annoyance, boredom, and melancholy. You may want to experiment with this yourself and practice a day or two of clean eating (increasing consumption of life-filled fruits and vegetables while forgoing coffee, sugar, and alcohol) to see if you laugh more.

Aside from physical clarity, mental clarity is important. STOP THINKING for heaven's sake! We, in this culture, are so preoccupied with our own thoughts that the pure energy of laughter just lies there dormant much of the time. Part of the reason that children are so magical is that they live in the present. Have you ever noticed how much they laugh? It is wonderfully contagious.

Laughter can be viewed as feedback that you are doing the right thing—connecting to your core, managing your energy by setting appropriate boundaries, regularly clearing your head and body, and cultivating your passions by doing what you love. Laughter is a byproduct of energized living.

For some reason there is an unspoken rule that, as adults, we have to be serious most of the time. Yes, some of the time it's appropriate, but don't you think most of us take life a bit too seriously in general? Being filled with energy makes us lighter than the average Joe or Josephine. This is good—too much heaviness or seriousness bogs us down, inhibiting laughter. Being light helps us to flow through life fairly effortlessly, and when things go wrong, we simply adjust course and flow another direction. Life's too short to be excessively heavy. Laughter is the ultimate joyful lightness.

What makes you laugh? Is it watching your pet do cute things? Is it renting funny movies, or being around light-hearted people? Think for a moment about what tickles your funny bone. It may inspire you to have some fun.

Energy Tip: Right now, this very moment, think of the funniest movie you have ever seen. Go back to the first time you saw it and remember how you felt. Notice your belly rise and fall as waves of energy move up your body in response to the hilarity of it all.

Some of us do laughter really well, some of us express love abundantly, some are gifted with empathy and do not shy away from genuine sadness. Each emotion is another face of the same essential energy. To be fully energized we need to be able to feel all the variations of life. If you are a laugher—brilliant! Share your joy with others.

If you find that you have laughers around you, but you do other emotions better, vow, as my sister did, to get in touch with your inner clown. Commit to at least one bout of serious laughter each day. The intention is all that is required. You will be pleasantly surprised as situations spontaneously present themselves and you respond with genuine heartfelt laughter.

Pleasure

Europeans understand something that Americans are still learning: the art of refined pleasure. They know how to enjoy a single cup of smooth coffee in a small, beautiful, porcelain cup with a matching saucer. Americans go for vente lattes. Europeans customarily eat four small meals throughout the day—Americans head for the buffet and make sure they get their money's worth. When I was growing up, my father frequently talked about some neighbors he had as a boy. "Everything they did was big!" he would tell us kids. "They took me out for my first pizza pie...." Legendary stories of big cups, big servings of food, big stomachs, and most importantly, their big hearts, filled our home. Despite my father's fondness for this family, they represent a part of American culture that is not healthy. Overindulging in anything diminishes the ability to experience pleasure.

Today, I am writing outside at a coffee shop. October in the Southwest is beautiful. It is around 70 degrees and the sky is bright blue. There is a small fountain of bubbling water in front of me and a tall, white, mission-looking building behind it. Every few moments, I look up, take a breath, and absorb the beauty.

Pleasure is what happens when you step out of auto-pilot and experience whatever is in front of you. It some-times seems elusive and hard to come by. I think this is because a layer of busy-ness covers our experiences of pleasure the way caramelized sugar covers crème brulee. It takes only a slight tap of a spoon to get to the good stuff.

Available to you each moment, pleasure promises to transport you to another world. It is the world that children and animals inhabit. When we take off our blinders and enter this world, colors are brighter, flavors are richer, and love is more palpable.

I believe that enjoying life through the senses is one of our obligations as human beings. And that, if we choose to pass on the thousands of opportunities pleasure has to offer each day, regret will follow. Every time I watch

The Color Purple, I am moved to tears during the beautiful scene in which "Sug" declares, "I think it pisses God off if you walk by the color purple in a field and don't notice it...."

Aside from the pure "pleasure" of pleasure, you receive a healthy dose of spiritual energy each time you dip your spoon into the creamy custard.

I can hear you now: "If I dip my spoon into the custard I will burst out of my pants!" Here's my question to you: Do you think that if you really enjoy life's simple pleasures, that you will become obese?

When a bottle of wine replaces a single glass with dinner, or a candy bar takes the place of a square of fine dark chocolate, pleasure is not the goal—pumping energy is.

Mindless consumption is a subconscious search for self. We lose ourselves and life becomes a chase. We all have a desire to move forward in life, but when our attention becomes too focused on the future, so does our energy. Where does this leave you in the here and now?

Energy Tip: Dedicate an afternoon to pleasure. Discover the pleasure in everything you do: breathing, eating, walking, or working. At the end of the day, notice how you feel.

Pleasure is nourishing in a juicy, lubricating way. It seeps into the cracks and crevices of your being and acts as a moisturizing balm. As you change your orientation from racing through life to enjoying it, you will find your skin plump with life and your eyes glistening with moisture.

Tuning in to your surroundings enhances pleasure. If it sounds Zen-like, it is. Pleasure is grounded in mindfulness. Perhaps for us puritan, hard-working Americans, a paradigm shift is in order. Consider pleasure to be an indication that you are floating on the current of your own energy—an indication that you are living fully rather than partially.

Taking pleasure in everything absolves us of the need to over-consume anything. Choosing to taste, smell, feel, see, and hear our surroundings is the ultimate inside-out nourishment. Enjoy!

Chapter 7
Look to the Future

We have now explored the spiritual, emotional, mental, and physical levels of self. We plugged into our spiritual cores, allowing the energy to clear out old emotions and mental patterns, ultimately penetrating our physical bodies and beyond.

Now we take a look at another, more subtle-level system: the seven energy centers of the body. We've learned to manage our energy in a practical way, which supports our growth in the world. Spiritual evolution also involves the sequential awakening of each of these seven energy centers. As we learn the lessons of each center, energy flows upward, beginning to open the next center. Layer after layer opens like petals of a flower, until, ultimately, we are in full bloom.

In this final section, practical gives way to mystical as we cultivate seven life-enhancing inner attributes. Each attribute corresponds to one of the seven major energy centers of the body and is paired with an affirmation that, when repeated, facilitates the opening of that center. You may repeat one affirmation a day for each day of the week, or choose to focus on one at a time for as long as needed. As you affirm the statement affiliated with a particular energy center, you will open and release any blocks, thereby increasing your overall energy capacity even more.

Just as your outer world is an extension of your inner world, the future is an extension of the present. The current form of your life—your body and external circumstances—is a delayed reflection of your internal orientation or way of approaching the world. Through time, the way you inwardly process the world around you creates energy patterns that dictate your experience with the outer world. Therefore, if you want to have a different form or physical experience in the future, you will want to change your inner landscape now.

Upon completion of this final section you will be open and energized—truly bright. From this place, you radiate goodness. In addition to bringing much-needed light into the world, the intense spiritual energy that you embody acts as a magnetic force field, allowing you to attract the life of your dreams. Your preferences and desires, however, remain light and unattached (literally) to any specific outcome. By now, you realize that nothing external can replace the true nourishment that flows from your own essence. You remain inwardly focused, carefully monitoring your vital energy.

Becoming attuned to the power of your own essence has helped you realize how quickly you become diluted and un-magnetized when you poorly utilize your energy or try to control external circumstances. This energy—your essence—now resides within you and naturally flows through you as you find yourself at peace and in love with life.

Contained in each of your goals and dreams are energetic qualities that you desire. Perhaps you yearn to feel grounded, secure, or inspired. Achievement alone will not provide you with these qualities, but choosing to embrace these qualities will lead to fulfillment beyond your dreams.

The following is a chart of the seven inner attributes that support the flow of life, and the outcomes you will experience as each energy center opens and clears.

Attribute	Affirmation	Outcome
Grounding	I AM GROUNDED	Security and Growth
Creativity	I AM CREATIVE	Desire and Pleasure
Empowerment	I AM EMPOWERED	Strength and Self-Esteem
Love	I AM LOVING	Openness and Connection
Expression	I AM EXPRESSIVE	Fulfillment and Discipline
Insight	I AM INSIGHTFUL	Vision and Guidance
Inspiration	I AM INSPIRED	Enlightenment and Miracles

I AM GROUNDED

Grounding is essential, fostering a sense of security and providing a platform for growth. As stated earlier, many of us have deep-seated fears of being homeless or without the means for basic survival. When present, this fear is often covered in layers of over-consumption and distraction. Survival fears are an indication that your sense of security is externally based, which leads to a quandary because external reality is constantly changing. Grounding yourself in your spiritual nature is to create a solid foundation from which to "build your house." Cultivating this inner foundation allows you to transcend fears about survival and security, and gradually opens this *energy center*, which is located at the base of the spine. Ultimately you experience a profound sense of internal security and freedom.

If you worry about the safety of yourself or your loved ones, or about issues related to food, shelter, or "not having enough," you will want to pay particular attention to cultivating a sense of being grounded. When feeling fearful, your energy center at the *base of your spine* constricts, causing your overall system to weaken.

Affirmation: I AM GROUNDED

Along with affirming, "I AM GROUNDED," it is useful to ground yourself daily. This is a practical matter, and physical in nature. Sitting meditation is grounding. You may even want to visualize roots extending through the base of your spine deep into the earth, allowing calm, serene, and stable energy to fill your being.

Taking a walk outside and focusing on your feet as they touch the ground is also grounding. Plants, dirt, daily routines, and rituals are grounding. People with waif-like bodies, or those who "live in the clouds" will want to make sure that they ground themselves daily to evenly distribute the energy throughout their bodies, and not "blow away" during a stormy time or be "knocked over" by an unpredictable event.

Along with daily grounding rituals, security and safety fears can sometimes be processed by allowing yourself to mentally challenge the validity of the fear every time it surfaces, or even just to play it out in your mind. If your biggest fear is being assaulted and you can't shake it by realistically evaluating the chance of it occurring, you might want to imagine what it would be like if it did happen. What would you do? How would you handle it? If you allow yourself to contemplate the fear, rather than act as though it doesn't exist, some of the pent-up energy may loosen and dissipate, making space for grounding energy to take its place.

You can also mentally affirm the truth of your security. The essence of who you are is secure regardless of how much money you have or what your living conditions are. Energy cannot be destroyed,—even death does not destroy our essence; we simply move to a different locale.

The stronger your relationship is with the unseen, purely energetic aspect of yourself, the more conviction you'll have that you cannot be harmed. Along with grounding rituals, playing out the worst-case scenario, and affirming the truth of your security, you will want to continue cultivating a relationship with the unseen or energetic levels of yourself. As energy fills the lower regions of your body, you will become more grounded. Daily tending keeps you this way as you move on to explore other aspects of your life, loves, and passions.

The color associated with this energy center is *red*. You intuitively know when you need to ground yourself. On those days you can wear red, choose a red coffee mug, or visualize the color moving through your body. Grounding leads to stability, growth, and abundance. Grounding into the earth and celebrating the physical security that it provides supports this energy center, allowing it to relax and open.

As the center opens, fears may wash over you as they release. You may have a bad dream or two. This is positive. Allow the center to clear itself of anything that diminishes its capacity to do its job. If you already feel grounded, secure, and abundant, simply affirm this reality a couple of times, and then move on to the next energy center. Otherwise, repeat this affirmation as long as you desire, and it will lead to feeling safe and secure.

As Abraham Maslow (the American psychologist who taught about the hierarchy of needs) suggested, when we do not feel secure, all our energy goes toward trying to protect ourselves and to filling this basic need. Only when we experience an unwavering sense of security from within, is life energy free to move to higher levels of expression.

I AM CREATIVE

As energy moves up your body it naturally wants to extend itself. Humans have an innate desire to leave an imprint on the world through children and other contributions. When life moves through you from the inside out, everything that you do is creative. In a very real way, we are born to create.

Creativity initially takes the form of desire. The seeds of desire take root in the second energy center of the body located below your belly button. This center is tied to the sexual organs, the center of procreation. Desire moves energy up the body, where it becomes further refined to the point of expression.

Acknowledging that our desires are natural and healthy help open this energy center. As you affirm, "I AM CREATIVE," you may also want to add the variations, "I AM SEXUAL," or "I DESIRE." The feelings of desire to create and extend beyond ourselves are primal and somewhat unrefined at this level.

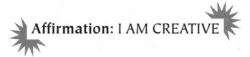 **Affirmation:** I AM CREATIVE

The color associated with this center is *orange*. Delight in this fun color every time you feel the need to tap in to this primal energy source, feeding the creative juices within you.

As this area of your body begins to relax and expand, you may find yourself feeling restless with desire. You may want to write down the thoughts and feelings that surface. It is important to keep the energy moving through your system so that self-defeating patterns do not develop. One of the best things you can do to support energy flow is physical exercise. Aerobic exercise does a fantastic job of moving energy through the body, and is a brilliant way to transmute raw desire when immediate gratification is calling.

Some become stuck at this level attempting to feed the bottomless pit of unrefined desire and passion. It is here that patterns of overindulgence take hold, becoming addictive or self-defeating. Identifying and working toward that which we wish to create on a higher level also helps the energy continue to move upward. Here we focus on what we want rather than what we don't want. For example, rather than saying, "I no longer want to have empty sex for instant gratification…," one might say, "I choose meaningful relationships that nurture my soul." As our positive desires become energized, our essence naturally seeks to fulfill them.

We evolve on spiritual and energetic levels as we master the tasks of each of these centers, allowing the energy to continuously move up the body until total integration is achieved. Creating health in this energy center is facilitated when we acknowledge the creative and desirous nature of our being. This gloriously passionate center is the seat of pleasure. Life would be dull without it. Actually, there wouldn't be any life at all without the primal desire arising from this energy center.

I AM EMPOWERED

A strong and open inner core is essential for those of us committed to brightness. We become empowered as we connect to our cores, allowing them to transform us from within. Internally derived power can never be taken away. One can give it away if one chooses, but once this point of personal evolution has been attained, giving it away is unlikely.

The seat of empowerment resides in your *abdomen or solar plexus*. This is the area that you clutch when someone says something mean-spirited in an attempt to "take a piece" of you. It is the abdomen that we seek to cover while around people we don't trust. It is also the part of the body that warns you with a "gut feeling" when something is not right. The color associated with this energy center is *yellow* like the sun. Yellow brightens our day, provides essential core nourishment, and transforms energy into a refined version, which ultimately becomes your power source.

We've all experienced what it feels like to be empowered. To get that feeling now, focus on your breathing. Notice your abdomen rise and fall as you calmly take another breath. Visualize abundant energy in your body, rather than dangling strings attached to the various things and people in your life. This calm, connected, open, and energized state is what empowerment feels like.

We become authentically empowered when using will to channel raw desires upward. When you willfully choose not to give into immediate gratification arising from the first two energy centers (impulsive pleasure seeking), this center ignites, producing the feeling of tension that burns off any undisciplined patterns. Our impulsive tendencies are then replaced with refined power. This process is fundamental to energy management.

When we do not engage the powerful will of this center to refine our primal desires, we feel powerless and our self-esteem suffers.

It is going through the fire that delivers us to ourselves. Each time you abstain from what you know doesn't support your overall well-being, and surrender to the uncomfortable feeling associated with restraint, you build a strong character and constitution in a very real way.

In addition to refining lower desires, your transformative core helps achieve a healthy level of detachment from anything that is not your true source of energy. Any wound left unhealed, any person or situation you try to control, anything you obsess about or are addicted to, spreads your energy thin, resulting in a loss of personal power.

Reclaiming your energy from these outside sources starts the embers burning, creating physical tension. At that point the strings or cords extending from your body detach from these various objects (or people) of desire and reintegrate into your being. The reason the objects became so desired in the first place is that you have imbued them with your energy—take it back!

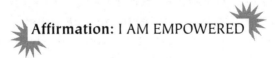

Affirmation: I AM EMPOWERED

Affirming your naturally empowered state supports this process of reintegration. When empowered (filled with our own essence), Your power of attraction gets stronger and we become highly magnetic. It is from this place that we attract that which we desire. The key is to remain detached from your desires, simply thinking of them as preferences, because if you over-attach, you will lose your power. If this skill of maintaining a desire without attachment were made into a video game, kids would learn the delicate balance at an early age!

The process is the outcome. Life is happening right now, and to give away your energy, love, inner peace, or any other life-enhancing state in the pursuit of a dream, is idolatry.

Those of you who have mastered the art of attracting your desires understand that balancing desire with a healthy level of detachment is essential. Everything we receive in the physical world is simply icing on the cake, not to be compared with the bliss that comes from remaining open to life.

True self-esteem results from authentic empowerment. As we strive to keep our focus on remaining energized, rather than on external situations, identity tends to shift to a more stable, internally derived sense of self. You are powerful. As you look at the areas of your life explored in this book and gently bring the pieces of yourself back into your body, your life will explode with magic.

I AM LOVING

Located *near your heart* is the energy center of love. As energy moves up the body, it often encounters a fortress of protection around this area. Opening your heart center is one of the most fulfilling things you can do for yourself. Love is the ultimate source of nourishment.

Buddha taught compassion—an attribute of the heart. If you are hard on yourself or others, if you have experienced heartbreak recently (or not so recently), or if you find yourself in an unkind setting at home or work, this energy center is likely constricted. As you open your heart center you cultivate the inner attribute of expansion— the state of being that allows you to truly open up to yourself and others.

As has been previously stated in this book, if you are in the midst of emotional toxicity—anything other than compassion and kindness—you are losing energy. Hopefully you are surrounded by compassion, kindness, and patience. If you are not, please look at how to "clean up" your environment so that your heart feels safe enough to expand.

Who do you love? What do you love? When was the last time you felt overwhelmed with love and compassion? The feeling of love expands as energy moves from your core and up through your heart center. The color associated with this center is *green,* a color known for its healing properties.

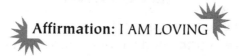

Affirmation: I AM LOVING

Your *heart* is the fourth energy center from both directions. Located in the middle, this center has the ability to balance your entire system, or to create severe blocks. Focusing on compassion for yourself and others not only opens your heart center, but affects the other centers as well. For example, when you choose compassion, judgments of the mind naturally fall away. Variations of this affirmation include, "I AM LOVING," "I AM LOVED," and "I LOVE." Choose whatever phrasing feels right to you.

If you feel that your heart center is constricted, you'll want to start by having compassion and love for yourself. If you feel a "failure" in any way, commit to forgiving yourself. Find a way to reframe your actions as a growth opportunity for yourself or others. Maybe you neglected a child, and through the experience the child became strong and unstoppable. Whatever the situation, forgiveness opens the doors to love. Once you can feel compassion for yourself, this will naturally extend to others. Keep it going and soon you will feel bathed in love.

Remaining energetically open rather than constricted keeps us well energized and enables our future to unfold more rapidly. More energy in your system equals more magnetic attraction. Your heart center is the focal point for remaining open. You may want to reread the Follow Your Heart section for ideas on how to continually open your heart.

We have embraced *the physical dimension* of our existence through grounding to the earth and the root of our being, so that we may grow in all areas of our life. We have connected to our *creative center* where we get in touch with the desire to leave our unique imprint on the world. We've integrated the fragmented aspects of ourselves back into our *power center* so that we may experience our energy as more present-focused, and therefore approach each moment empowered. Now we open ourselves to life by *living in love.*

The next three energy centers are the centers of *expression* (throat), *insight* (third eye) and *inspiration* (top of the head). As energy moves up your body, each of these centers becomes more open and activated, rushing nourishment and energy into your entire body.

I AM EXPRESSIVE

We all reach a point at which we feel a strong urge to express our essence. For many of us, the trials and tribulations of life cause us to withhold our thoughts, feelings, and creations out of a fear of being judged, or worse yet, rejected. Some even forget that they have anything to say.

Words are only one level of expression, yet they are powerful. Words transport energy, moving it from your being into the minds and hearts of others. Each word is like a little vehicle, taking on the essence of what the communicator is trying to express. Finding the right word or vehicle to transport your expression is an art form, and well worth the effort it takes to cultivate.

Our task as Bright Ones is to be bold enough to express our essence, for if fear holds us back, we become dull. The story at the beginning of the book about the man with radiating energy illustrates that self-expression goes well beyond words. We express ourselves loudly through demonstration, without saying a word. And if we try to hide our essences by using words that don't match our thoughts and feelings, others know.

One of my all-time favorite quotes is by Ralph Waldo Emerson. He succinctly captured this concept when he said, "What you are speaks so loudly I cannot hear what you say."

The current theme of my Website is "Express Yourself." Here's why: You can do everything recommended in this book to bring energy into your body and manage it efficiently so that you do not become drained, but if you don't express your essence, your energy gets backed up like a clogged sink. If you express it in a compromised way, only sharing the "positive" stuff or expressions of which you think others will approve, energy becomes twisted up inside you and your overall expression is diluted and distorted.

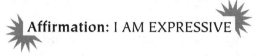

Affirmation: I AM EXPRESSIVE

The energy center associated with self-expression is the *throat*. The color is bright *blue*. As you affirm, "I am expressive," notice yourself wearing only the clothes that reflect who you are, saying words that you really mean, and finding a passionate pursuit to carry your essence into the world. Wear or surround yourself with blue when you feel the need to cultivate your ability to express yourself. I find it interesting that this has been my favorite color for the last several years. You will find that you are drawn to the various colors associated with each energy center when they need opening. Your intuition will direct you.

I'm sure you've noticed that when you are true to yourself and express that truth, you feel fulfilled. This is because self-expression completes the energy cycle. You first receive nourishment through daily spiritual practice. You then manage your energy by setting appropriate boundaries and taking impeccable care of yourself. Finally, you express yourself, making room to receive fresh, vital energy.

It is the fresh energy that comes into your system as you continuously express yourself that fulfills you. The golden nugget revealed with increased self-expression is that you become so nourished that any addictive behaviors simply fall away. Addictive behaviors are unconscious attempts to bring energy into your body. However, expressing your essence is ultimately so fulfilling that you won't want to risk the enhanced feeling you experience by over consuming anything.

We are expressive beings. If you are a quiet person who loves to paint, that is your unique brand of self-expression. If you are a wild extrovert with a red convertible—go for it, have a blast. Be yourself, love yourself, and always express yourself.

I AM INSIGHTFUL

Insight is available to everyone. It is in you whether you heed it or not, always there waiting for you to listen. Your *third eye*, the *center of your forehead*, is the area of insight. As we focus on opening this energy center, we increase our ability to see. Some become clairvoyant, while others cultivate sharp minds that routinely operate beyond the chatter of routine, obsessive thinking.

Insight is the voice of life. It is associated with a bigger picture, and is eager to guide you on even the smallest decisions of your day. As each energy center in your body opens, energy rises up through your being and into your mind. Information imbedded in spiritual energy is available when we still our minds long enough to perceive it.

The absence of true insight is neurosis. The metaphor that always comes to me when I think of life without spiritual guidance is that of a cat chasing its own tail. Round and round it goes making no progress at all without realizing the futility of its pursuit.

You know when you tap into insight and wisdom because your whole body feels engaged as you perceive it. A deep-down feeling of conviction resides in your belly, and your mind becomes quiet. It is as if a message awaits you at the bottom of a still, clear lake. There are no waves and whirlpools—just stillness, peace, and whole body resonance.

Being bright in this information age requires that you tap into your own source of insight. Feel free to gather information, do research on the Internet, or ask others for advice, but, when it is time to make a decision, allow your own wisdom to guide you. Only you know what is right for you.

It takes practice to develop the ability to tap into your inner wisdom at will. As you know, telling your mind, "Stop thinking!" does not work. However, daily practice of dropping your awareness down into your body and connecting to your breath yields seconds of mental stillness. These mere seconds take some of the compacted mental energy and redistribute it throughout your body. Eventually you will find that all you need to do to still your mind is connect with your breath.

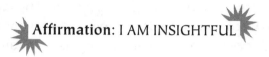

Affirmation: I AM INSIGHTFUL

As you affirm, "I AM INSIGHTFUL," the area around your third eye will relax and open, helping you connect with your inner guidance. The color associated with this energy center is *indigo*. You may want to visualize a beautiful night's sky in your third eye to help this area open. If you find that you're having difficulty stilling your mind long enough to perceive guidance, try putting one hand on your forehead and another on your abdomen to balance and connect the energy.

Your inner wisdom is here to reveal a vision of you at your brightest. Embrace this vision. Look at it every day. Commit to walking toward it, one step at a time. The world needs you to be energized and fulfilled. As each one of us marches toward brightness, others become inspired. Happiness brings light into the world. Do not hesitate; listen to yourself and *trust*. Sometimes the guidance is faint at first; it is a hunch or a deep-down whisper. Just noticing it and contemplating it will help bring it to the surface. Other times the guidance doesn't seem to make sense. Try to remember that your view is limited, and that, in time, the bigger picture will reveal itself.

The opening of this energy center is very freeing. What a relief to know that we don't have to over-think every detail of life. In fact, under-thinking is the way to go! All we need to do to live the best life possible, one in which we embrace our spiritual, emotional, mental, and physical potential, is to put life in charge. As my innocent daughter says every time she completes something she's nervous about, "That was so easy!"

I AM INSPIRED

The more infused you are with spiritual energy, the more mysterious life becomes. The *seventh energy center* resides at the *top of your head above your third eye*. Miracles arrive as your essence reaches upward toward the heavens.

Inspired means *in spirit*—filled with energy, in other words: enlightened. As life tingles within and through your body, the world transforms. You find meaning, purpose, support, guidance, self-love, and security. This would be enough, but there is more.

A Course in Miracles states, "There is no order of difficulty in miracles." What we know, and increasingly experience as Bright Ones, is that matter is nothing more than condensed energy. As we lighten up by releasing the blocks to natural self-expression, the energy within us becomes less dense and more malleable.

At the center of insight we learned to dispel our lower-level thoughts in favor of higher guidance; this takes the lid off our potential. Now, at the seventh level, we dare to expect miracles. Never again will you have a mundane day. Once energy reaches this level, you have clearly put life in charge. The final step is further surrender, allowing life to usher in a reality beyond your wildest dreams.

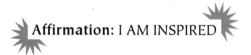

Affirmation: I AM INSPIRED

The color associated with this energy center is *purple*. All the beautiful shades of purple help us feel connected to our spiritual nature. As you affirm, "I am inspired," you support life taking you a step further than you've ever been. Don't stop now, it's just getting exciting.

Inspired by love, Luther Vandross sang, "Little miracles happen every day...." Watch as mystery takes hold of your life, presenting twists and turns that amuse and enliven your spirit.

We are at the point in our exploration of personal energy management where words fall short. Describing the exhilarating quality of inspiration is difficult. You know—you have felt it. At this level, we commit to having this elusive feeling as a part of our daily lives.

As this book draws to an end, I would like to leave you with a final vision: Picture everyone in the world as vibrant, sparkly, and embodying their unique face of spirituality. Some are lovey, some are bouncy, some are wise, and some are witty. All are gorgeous and life-filled. Mother Earth is luscious and green. She no longer cries. We all dance around and enjoy our creations as we love each other and ourselves. From each of us pours the brightest, purest light you can imagine. Anyone struggling is bathed in this light until they are strong enough to re-connect with their own.

All this and more is possible. Be in joy as you move toward brightness, for, in truth, you're already there.

Index

About the Author

For more than 15 years, Kimberly has studied the principles of embodied spirituality and healing. In her work as a psychotherapist and energy coach, Kimberly teaches how to transform draining patterns, thereby bringing more light into one's body and surrounding world. Her first book, *Opening to Life: Reconnecting with Your Internal Source of Energy, Wisdom, and Joy* received both Editor's Choice and Reader's Choice awards. *www.kimberlykingsley.com*